THE

UNEASY

MAN

A REALISTIC APPROACH TO OVERCOMING ANXIETY, STOPPING YOUR WORRY & BUILDING AUTHENTIC CONFIDENCE

GREG RIDER

Greg Rider

TABLE OF CONTENTS

PREFACE

I want to start this book off by asking you to think back on life and isolate your very *lowest* point. When did you most feel life was against you and that it couldn't get any worse?

I want you to relive that moment, just for a couple of minutes.

Maybe that moment was in high school, college or university, or when you graduated and entered the "real" world . It could have been a couple of years ago, a couple of months ago or. maybe, you're going through it right now.

It's in that moment when we think to ourselves:

"There *must* be more to life than this…"

You're tired of beating your head against the wall. You're tired of playing small and you're starving for some clarity in your life.

"THE UNEASY MAN" is the survival guide. It's YOUR book, and it will help you build up your confidence and help silence those voices in your head: the ones that keep telling you that you are not good enough to live the life of your dreams.

In this book, I will give you the best advice I can - advice that took me years to learn and that I wish I had when I was at my lowest point.

The Uneasy Man

DISCLAIMER:

I am not a doctor or a psychiatrist and I do not have any interest in becoming either. I am simply a man that wants to help you improve your self-confidence and overcome your worry and anxiety.

Growing up in my generation is nothing like the generations that preceded us - our parents or grandparents. We have to realize that we are not looking to just "get a job, pay the bills and drink on weekends with friends." We want more, we want to make a difference and we want to create a life we are proud of.

We have the ability to be whoever we want: it has never been easier to start a blog, create a website or online business, or even get noticed for your artistic abilities via the internet. The only thing that is stopping you from creating your dream life is that imaginary box that you are living in: that thing called your "comfort zone" that you too afraid to step out of because you may fail or get hurt.

Living your entire life in this little box will haunt you when you become a middle-aged man or woman looking back on your life, wishing that you *did more*.

This book is aimed at men and women aged 16 - 25 because that's who I relate with best. At first, I wrote this book for men, but I eventually changed that because this book is for everyone. I have chapters in this book that are directed at men, but I want women to read this as well. Not because it will help you understand a man's psyche better, but because it will show you the kinds of things that men think about and it will give you a better understanding of what a man must go through in order to achieve self-confidence.

This book will help anyone that has suffered from depression, anxiety or worry.

Just remember that wherever you are in your life right now, it's never too late to make a change for the better. You could quit your job, break up with your girlfriend or boyfriend and just go travelling.

I hope this book helps to build your confidence so you can have more love, more freedom, and more connection in your life.

I wrote this book because I never want another young person to have to go through the self-inflicted pain that I endured. I wish someone would have put their hand on my shoulder when I was at my lowest point and said, "here, read this." However, if that had happened, I wouldn't have needed to write this book, so in a way I'm thankful that I was able to discover so much about myself even though I felt very alone during the process.

INTRODUCTION

My name is Greg Rider Farrell and I am a 26 year-old man who was born in Ontario, Canada.

This is my *lowest* point:

When I was 21, I walked away from a six-car accident that changed my life forever.

I was driving home from an internship in Toronto when I pulled off the highway to grab a coffee before merging back on. I was in the fast lane driving 80km/h. I looked down for a moment to turn up the volume on my favourite song. As I looked up, I noticed the car in front of me wasn't slowing down. It was stopped. I hit the brakes and in an instant I slid into the back of the car. At the last second, I swerved so I wouldn't hit the trunk. I had no seatbelt on. I held myself in the car by locking my elbows and holding on for dear life. I blacked out when my head smashed into the steering wheel and when I came to, my car was covered in black smoke. I thought I was on fire so I immediately jumped out of the car and screamed, "WHAT HAPPENED?" A lady walked up behind me and told me that everyone was okay, and that I was just involved in a six-car crash. It was a domino effect and I was the last one in. My car was a write-off. After the crash, I didn't move from my bed for four days. I wasn't injured, but the question that kept coming up in my mind was: "What If I died? How would people remember me?" I became depressed contemplating this.

Greg Rider

I knew instantly I would not be remembered how I *wanted* to be remembered. The idea that people's memory of me wouldn't represent the legacy of the person I wanted to be led me to a dark and dreadful place. I contemplated not going back to my internship - just running away and never coming back. At one point, ending my life crossed my mind. I wasn't serious about it, but it did cross my mind. I knew I didn't have the "courage" to do that to myself. I couldn't do that to my family and friends, so I had to do something that most people are too afraid to do: I had to change. After four days of laying in my bed I finally mustered up the courage to go back to my internship so I could graduate college and get on with my life.

The crash was my defining moment. It was the darkest time in my life and I felt completely alone. I had my friends and family, but I felt no one could understand the thoughts that rushed through my mind. I felt no one could relate and there was something seriously wrong with me.

I didn't want a normal life. I wanted to push the envelope. I wanted to be proud of what I had accomplished. I wanted to live and leave a legacy for my future children and grandchildren. What I want is to make an impact on my generation and talk about what I went through and something we all deal with - the struggle to find ourselves.

After the crash, I made a commitment to myself: I would dedicate my life to my dream of being on stage, entertaining and inspiring others through my stories and music. I had no idea how I was going to get there, but I knew I was never going to give up my efforts in achieving that goal.

MARK MY WORDS.

1. Describe Your Perfect Day

The best way to predict your future is to create it.
- Abraham Lincoln

Have you ever felt like you were drifting through life with no direction?

Have you ever thought that if you knew exactly what the future held, it would be easier to build a roadmap towards it?

Have you ever felt like planning for your future took you away from "living in the moment?"

If so, I'm right there with you. I have felt the exact same way.

After the car accident I discovered personal development. I didn't know much about the industry, including how popular and incredible it is. I assumed it was corny and impractical, but that was because I knew nothing about it.

I was killing some time at a bookstore in Toronto waiting for my boss to pick me up and take me to work, since I was without a car. I started walking through the aisles, coffee in hand and I found myself in the "Self Help" section. I had never been there before.

Greg Rider

I came across a book entitled *Stop Worrying & Start Living* by Dale Carnegie. The book's cover was so vibrant and colourful that it literally leapt off the shelf.

This book was exactly what I needed in my life. I had so many questions about so many things, but no answers at all.

After flying through that book I was itching for more. The next book I picked up was *Success Principles* by Jack Canfield. He was the one of the co-creators of 'Chicken Soup for the Soul,' a collection of short stories that will either make you cry, laugh or think beyond convention. He created these books targeting human emotion as a way to revolutionize people's views on the treatment of others. With stories pertaining to basic principles like empathy, suffering and taking responsibility for your actions, he was able to create a very inspiring way to show resiliency and belief in something that other people might not see at the time.

I can relate to this because when I describe my dream, people don't see it working out the way I do. They often think it's a little farfetched and that I need to be more realistic. I've never been a fan of "being realistic." Not long from now, when you see me on stage inspiring thousands of people with stories and music, some will draw conclusions as to how I got there. They will think I've always had the natural ability to be on stage and this is what I was born to do. Most people will only see the tip of the iceberg and not the hundreds of hours I've spent working on honing my craft. This book is just a chunk of that iceberg.

The Uneasy Man

I believed in myself when no one else did and I refused to settle for a job that was "good enough."

Canfield's book, *Success Principles,* really got me thinking about my direction and my ideal day. He will ask you to answer questions about your ideal day, which made me anxious because I felt I was dreaming too big. You have to allow yourself to dream. One day, I will have a place in California with a view of the ocean. At times I still don't feel I deserve that. However, I decided to write down anything and everything that came to my mind and not worry if it was unrealistic.

I just had to write it down. I pictured myself in my dream house, talking to my wife, driving my sports car to the coffee shop and travelling around the world performing. I visualized everything.

Many people think describing your perfect day is useless because you won't be focusing on the present day. The way I see it is you have to work backwards from your perfect day, all the way down to what you're going to do today, this week and next month. We will talk more about this in a later chapter.

Many people might think writing down your ideal life in too much detail is materialistic. The way I see it, writing down your ideal day in detail allows you envision it that much more, thus making it more attainable. You have to allow yourself to be very detailed in order for you to see the image clearly. Instead of visualizing any sports car, I specifically see myself driving a blue Audi R8 Spyder.

We will encounter people who can't do this because they think it's a waste of time, or it's simply a fantasy that won't come true. I have learned that you can't change people's' minds once they believe something so strongly. I don't have time to argue. Remember that you have every right to envision and create the life of your dreams. It's your life, no one else's.

Here are the steps YOU can take to get these results:
Take out a new page of paper or flip to a new page in your journal. Use a pen to write this down. You may want to type it, but it's better to write it out because writing is known to make a better connection in your brain.

Take a moment to settle yourself as you gear up for long-term success. I want you to close your eyes and think into the future, imagining you are waking up and all of your dreams have come true. You are living your ideal life, so jot down what comes to mind. What do you see?

Where do you wake up?
I want you to describe the room. What's the first thing you see when you open your eyes?

Who is beside you?
Are you happily married to a wife? Is there a girlfriend in your life? Are you bachelor that wakes up next to a different girl every weekend?

The Uneasy Man

What city are you in?

What town or city has stolen your heart? Are you back in your hometown or have you moved across the country? Perhaps you've moved across the world?

What's the first thing you do when you wake up?

Do you head straight to the coffee machine, do some exercise or grab a glass of water? Explain your morning routine the way you would want to it to play out.

What do you eat for breakfast?

Do you take the time to sit down, sip a coffee and enjoy a nice meal with the newspaper in hand, or do you grab a quick shake and head out the door?

How will you make money today?

Are you self employed or working for someone? What is your dream job?

What kind of car(s) are parked in your garage?

What car do you drive to work? Don't just say a "sports car." Tell me the make, model, colour and year.

What do you fill your day with?

What kind of things do you do in the day? Are you meeting with clients, playing golf, working away on the computer or making phone calls? I want to know what you do during the day. Do you sneak out through the day for a workout or lunch with your significant other?

What do you have for dinner?

After you finish your work day, what do you want for dinner? Do you have the money to eat at a fancy restaurant or do you enjoy coming home to your partner, making a nice meal and sipping wine by the fireplace?

What do you do after dinner?

After you've consumed your wonderful meal, how do you spend the rest of your evening? Do you go out for a drink, watch television, hang out with your partner, meet with some friends, go back to work?

ALERT: This is YOUR chance to describe your ideal day! Give yourself permission to dream.

Be sure to avoid these mistakes:

1) Not thinking big enough: don't convince yourself that writing this down is "unrealistic." Play BIG!

2) Not giving detailed answers and just playing on the surface: make this as vivid as you possibly can.

3) Stopping halfway and saying this is stupid. You're stretching your comfort zone by doing this and your brain just wants you to go back to where you're comfortable. Finish the task at hand. Don't quit!

Creating your ideal day is an amazing task and it will show you where you WANT to go. Imagine you let 10 years go by and you leave your life up to "whatever happens, happens."

Imagine the feeling if you could look back at this list and everything you wrote down came true. Imagine how you would feel.

Action Step:

Pull out that piece of paper and begin writing out your ideal life. Make the next 30 minutes your time to dream. Turn off social media, turn off your phone and focus on getting this task done.

I wanted the first chapter to be about looking into the future to give you an idea of the day you are working towards when all of your dreams come true and you are living your ideal life. By no means will this create the confidence you need to get there, but it's a great step.

The next chapter will be your chance to "toot your own horn." I don't want to talk about the things you are bad at. I want to talk about the things you are good at. That is what we will focus on!

2. Play To Your Strengths

"Every great dream begins with a dreamer. Always remember, you have within you the strength, the patience, and the passion to reach for the stars to change the world"
- Harriet Tubman

Have you ever said to someone, "I'm not really good at anything, I'm just doing my current job because it's making me money?"

Have you ever felt like you have many more weaknesses than strengths?

Have you ever just sat and thought to yourself, "the only thing I'm good at is not knowing what I'm good at?"

Same here. You get the notion that you have WAY too many weaknesses and not enough strengths and that's why you are not where you want to be in your life. Here's the truth about me:

I have always felt that my list of weaknesses was way longer than my list of strengths.

I would get so depressed thinking about what I'm **not** good at that I wouldn't even take the time to find the things that I am good at!

The Uneasy Man

I remember when I was in my senior year of high school, it was one of my most stressful years and I was only 18! I felt everyone else knew which school they wanted to go to or what trade they were going to pursue. I felt like everyone had an idea except for me. People thought I had a plan because I put on an act as if I had it all figured out, but really, I was freaking out and I felt I couldn't be honest with anyone because I felt people wouldn't believe me.

Bottling up my emotions - that was a strength of mine! That only made it worse and I began to get so pissed off at myself that I would lie awake every night trying to find out what I was going to do. I would hardly sleep and I would drag my feet into school the next day. I was so uneasy about my future that Instead of trying to figure it out, I would distract myself with video games and anything else that didn't let me think about my future.

I remember making an appointment with the guidance counselor and I told her "I have no clue what program I want to take." She asked me what my interests were and I told her speaking in front of people, speaking on camera and sports. She was the one that actually said, "what about Sports Broadcasting? There are some great courses in college around here." I thought that sounded like a pretty good idea because I love watching sports highlights and talking about sports. I thought that was the perfect job for me.

I began thinking about that idea, and I started to become a little happier. I would tell people that I was thinking of studying

Sports Broadcasting and they would say "Oh my God, I can *so* see you doing that!" I was beginning to feel more confident about my decision to study sports broadcasting. I knew it was too late to apply for school next year, and in addition, I wanted to play high school volleyball for one more year to hone my skills.

In our senior year, we had a really good volleyball team and we ended up making it to the provincials that year. We placed fourth and after our final game, the coach and athletic director from Niagara College scouted me and asked if I knew what I was doing for school the following year. I told him that I had no idea, but I would go back for my victory lap and decide later.

They told me to keep Niagara in mind because they would love to have me play on their team. I knew if I had one more year of practice, I could be ready to play volleyball in college.

During my post-graduation victory lap, my goal was to start improving my marks in a couple key classes. English was one of my worst subjects because I was horrible at sentence structure and grammar. I am thankful that there are people that get paid to edit or else this book would not have been finished. Big thanks to Eric Green for the editing.

I began looking into Television Broadcasting and I found out that there was a really good program at Niagara College. I thought it would be good to move away from home for college, just to gain some independence. I found out what needed to be done to apply for the program and I worked hard on the essay that was due. The broadcasting course was difficult to get into because hundreds of students applied, but they only took a select amount because they wanted a smaller class, allowing for more focus on hands on techniques rather than theory.

In this course, I was going to learn about Television Production, Presentation and Film. In the first year, we did all three topics and in the second year we had pick a major.

I chose presentation because I wanted to be in front of the camera, not behind it. There was an ongoing joke that the presentation students were just a "face" and production students were the people who weren't good looking enough to be in front of the camera. There was actually a big rivalry between production students and presentation students. You would think we would all be friends, but that wasn't the case in the first semester of second year. In the second semester, we began working together more and realizing that the other major wasn't that bad.

Second year was when things started to change for me. Being called a "Face" did not sit well with me. I didn't want to be known as someone who just looked good on camera and talked about sports. I didn't want to just read off a teleprompter. I was pretty cocky back in college because I was a varsity athlete and I started thinking that I was better than the program. I thought, "I'm supposed to do more with my life than just be a sports broadcaster."

This caused me to stop focusing on my grades and focusing more on volleyball, partying, hooking up with women and enjoying my time in college. My grades began to suffer because

I didn't want to be in the program anymore. I was back to my ways of doing anything that distracted me from figuring out my future. I wanted to do things that made me happy. I didn't want to work a job just to make money. I wanted to wake up every morning and play to my strengths, but how?

Many people think writing out your strengths is being narcissistic or cocky. The way I see it, you are writing out the things that you are interested in and want to learn more about.

Many people can't complete this assignment because they are trying to answer the question, "what am I a master at," rather than, "what would I enjoy getting better at?"

Many people can write way more weaknesses than strengths. This makes it a lot easier to talk yourself down than talk yourself up.

Here are the steps YOU can take to get these results:

Write Down Your Assets:

Take the next two minutes to write down all of your assets. I'm not talking about your house, car, motorcycle or anything like that. Write down all of the unique qualities and traits about yourself. Imagine you are running for president or prime minister and you are creating an advertisement or commercial. I want you to write down all of the things you would say about yourself. Do not hold back. Nobody will see this list but you!

Bring gratitude into your life.

Take the next two minutes and write out all the things that you are grateful for. I want you to aim for about 20 - 25 things that you are grateful for. We spend so much thinking about what we don't have that we forget what we do have in our lives right now.

Write down your memories:

I want you to think back on your life and pull out your top ten memories. They will either make you laugh, smile, cry or think. You may not believe me when I say this, but you do have TEN THINGS that have made you into the person you are today. Start writing them down.

These exercises will be read every morning for the rest of your life and you will continue to update these lists throughout your life as you increase your assets, gratitude and memories.

Action Step:

Take the next thirty minutes to finish these exercises and transfer them to a 3x5 card that you can keep in your wallet.

After this is done, you can move onto the next chapter. You will love waking each morning and completing these exercises because they will put you on the right foot for the day.

Now, that you have written out these exercises, it's time to start getting clarity on your purpose and trying to focus our energy into something we love. To be honest, finding my purpose took me years and I kept changing it. In the next chapter, I will enlighten you about my story and how I found my purpose and how you can find your's too. Let's dive in!

3. Find Your Purpose

"I work really hard at trying to see the big picture and not getting stuck in ego. I believe we're all put on this planet for a purpose, and we all have a different purpose...When you connect with that love and that compassion, that's when everything unfolds."
- Ellen Degeneres

Have you ever been at a social outing and froze when someone asks, "what do you do for a living?"

Have you ever felt that you have too many interests and you can't seem to find that one you want to go all in on?

Have you ever wanted to hone in on your purpose?

ME TOO!

Having someone ask me, "What do you do for a living" was the toughest question to answer.

That question was my kryptonite and I avoided places where people may ask me that.

Growing up, I LOVED sports. I played as many sports as I could fit into the year. I played hockey, soccer, lacrosse, basketball, cross country, snowboarding, volleyball, badminton, tennis and squash. I enjoyed playing different sports, but I could never find one that I wanted to go "all in" with. I guess some things never change because that indecisiveness followed me into high school.

I knew I wasn't university bound. Going to lectures at night didn't interest me and I wanted the teacher to know my name, not just my student number. I fully understand that there are smaller classes in university as well, but I felt university was way too broad for me and I needed something more specific. I'm not saying the university approach is the wrong path in life because for some people, it's the right move.

BUT it's not the only path you can take. You could learn a trade, be an entrepreneur, or go to a college and get a specialized diploma. Don't just go to university because everyone else is.

I couldn't afford to spend 30-40k on something I wasn't completely sold on.

I chose to take the college approach because at that point I knew what I wanted to do with my life and that was to become a sports broadcaster.

I liked how intensive the program was. Even though it was very challenging to balance volleyball and school sometimes, I tried my best. I improved in front of the camera and behind the mic and I loved when the big red light came on that read "LIVE ON AIR."

I told you in the previous chapter that second year was when things started to change, but now I will tell you what really made me second guess my future in broadcasting. One day when we were in the lecture room my instructor went on a rant about how tough the industry really is. You're probably thinking that it's weird for a professor to talk that way but I understand his reasoning now. He didn't want to teach people that weren't 100%. He wanted people that were completely serious that this was their future. He would always say, "if this course isn't for you then you know where the door is." Do you know how many times I looked at that door? I usually sat close to the door…just in case.

If you asked me if I was sold on the program in first year, I would have said HELL YES! Asking me in second year was very different. The jokes about presentation students being "just a face" got to me and maybe I did care way too much about what people though. I feel it tainted my college experience. I wasn't going to be a drop out though. Fuck that.

I wanted to finish the program so I could say I was a college graduate and not a quitter. In the third year of the program, we had to find an internship in the industry. The goal was to find somewhere where we would eventually get hired on full time. I didn't want to work in the industry, so why the hell would I be motivated to find an internship in the field?

All my peers were scouring the web looking for places to hire them. They were talking with their favourite teachers trying to get contacts in the industry. Every couple of weeks we would have to sit down with one of our mentors. They were teachers in the industry that you got along with best. They were there to help guide you towards an internship.

Greg Rider

I picked my radio teacher because I thought we got along well and I think he saw something in me that I didn't see yet. He could tell I was distracted from finding an internship because I would show up and I would have nothing. I would just sit there and talk about how much I didn't want to find an internship. He told me that if I didn't find one then I would have to finish a 10,000 word essay on a topic that they chose for me. That sounded like a nightmare. There was no way I was going to be forced to write a essay, I was committed to finding something.

Summer was just around the corner and some of the students found jobs in the industry or worked another job while spending the rest of their time looking for their internship. Me on the other hand, I didn't want to think about it. I wanted to be a 21 year old man, so I found a job bartending in Muskoka. I managed to get hired at a resort called the *Delawanna Inn*.

This resort was right on the water in a small town called Honey Harbour. I drove up there in my grandma's 1990 Buick Lesabre, which she gifted to me. I called it "The Beige Rocket." Our lodgings were cabins which we would share with two to three roommates that worked at the resort. I met my roommate, Evan, on the first day. He was a little older than me. He told me a couple months later that he really didn't like when we first met. I was the really cocky meathead that showed up in the white undershirt and a cowboy hat. I recently came across some videos I made of myself when I first showed up at the resort and I could easily tell why people didn't like me by my first impression.

The Uneasy Man

As the summer went on. I began to move away from that meathead exterior and just turned into the party guy that was always singing and playing guitar. That was the summer I started playing guitar more serious. I brought this cheap one up with me but one night I got drunk and smashed it. I bought a new one a couple weeks later and I treated this one way better. During the summer, we drank every night and most days. We were either drunk or hungover when we were working. We lived in cabins that were all attached and all the servers and bartenders lived there. It was easily the most enjoyable summer of my life and I will never forget it. I met some of my best friends that summer and we managed to stay in contact for a number of years. We have drifted apart now, but I'm sure if we all got back together, it would be just like old times.

The end of summer was fast approaching and I still didn't have an internship. I was convinced that I was going to be writing that essay, but then something incredible happened.

I was working at the bar one evening and this couple from Toronto walked up to my bar and sat down for a drink. They were the only people in the bar, so we struck up a conversation. At the resort, there were three different bars to work at. One was a day bar, the second one was the lounge bar above the dining room and the third bar was this late night bar that I was in at the time. The couple and I had such a riveting conversation that they told me they we're just going to follow me around to all the different bars. On the nights when I didn't work at the late bar, I would head down to their cabin for some drinks and singing. By the end of the weekend, we became good friends and I finally asked them what they did for a living.

The man was a production manager for a Television studio in Toronto. Crazy right? The funny thing was school started in about three weeks and our internships were due the first day of school. I told him about the internship I needed and he told me he would hire me. I was so excited that day because I wasn't going to forced to write an essay. I drove home from Muskoka with a big smirk on my face.

The internship was in Etobicoke, so luckily I didn't have to commute into downtown Toronto everyday by train. Instead, I drove. The Beige Rocket was gone. My dad was getting a new car, so he gave me his Nissan Altima. This car was a little safer.

After I was hired for the internship, I didn't talk with the guy who hired me for quite awhile. I don't think he had any idea what I was going to do when I started. He just wanted me to show up and we will figure out as we go. I was pretty much hired to do the things he didn't want to do. The guys in the office were all really outgoing and I enjoyed talking with them because they gave me a lot of knowledge and insight into the world of TV Production. The company was known for making commercials, corporate videos and TV shows. A couple famous people would come through the office. I met the guy the does all the voices in the Fido commercials and the host of Cash Cab. Also, The podcast "Humble & Fred" was recorded in the same building so I got to meet those guys and they actually brought me on their show one time to sing. I was nervous as all Hell. I even got to meet David Wilcox and hear him play Riverboat Fantasy LIVE. If you don't know him, he is an icon in Canada.

The Uneasy Man

At the internship, I usually filled my days with mundane tasks, taking care of their clients, pretending to be busy, making coffee and working on random personal projects. Some days I enjoyed it and other days I was so bored that I would just watch the clock.

The car crash I spoke about in the beginning happened about 2 months into this job. After the crash, I took a couple days off from work to collect myself. Since my car was a write-off, I had to take two trains and a bus to get to the internship. I was getting really tired of having to go into my internship. Even if these guys wanted to hire me on full time, I would have said no. The internship made me dislike the industry even more. I was tired of taking orders from people, but I knew I had to finish the internship, so I could pass the course.

Once the internship ended, I was so relieved. My life was even more confusing because I felt like I had just wasted 2.5 years of my life. I spent money on something that I didn't want to do and I was back at the beginning.

Many people think they have to know exactly what to do after high school. The way I see it, I had to try different avenues to find out what I **DIDN'T** want to do. That way I don't have regrets later in my life.

Many people get so frustrated when they don't know what to do, and getting the "what are you doing with your life" question makes them very anxious. The way I see it, when people ask me what I'm doing with life, I tell them "well, I know what I don't want to do."

Many people dread going places where they will see people from high school. The way I see it, if you have a clever way of answering those cookie cutter questions then it's really not that bad.

I created something called the "Bubble Exercise". I wish I had this back when I was in high school, but alas I only came up with the exercise a couple of years ago.

Here are the steps YOU can take to get these results:

Grab a piece of paper and write your name at the bottom of the page. This is your starting point. Make the page landscape for more room

Draw three to five circles around your name like this:

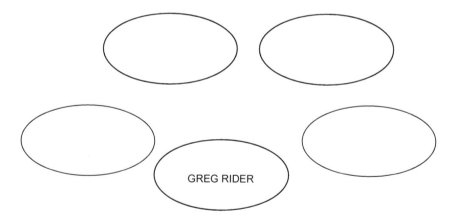

Write out a different interest in each circle:

The Uneasy Man

For example: TV Broadcasting, Sports, Marketing, Public Speaking

Start researching different jobs that are related to these interests. I want you come up with four or five different jobs for each interest. Google is your friend! Type in the jobs related to each interest and build a list.

After you have built your list for these interests, circle three that really interest you. Which of these jobs do you see yourself doing?

Research these jobs:

Find out what schooling you may need, how long it takes to get that position, annual salary etc. Look into the responsibilities that come with a job like that. Doing the research will show you if you actually feel passionate about this job or if you are just interested in the position title and the respect it comes with.

After you have done the research on the three jobs you circled, find the one that you want to concentrate on. This doesn't have to be the job that you do for the rest of your life, but at least it's a start! If it doesn't work out, go back to the drawing board and try the next one!

Be sure to avoid these mistakes:

→ Doing this all in your head and not writing this down on paper. Make it visual!

→ Thinking this exercise will find you the job you want to do for the rest of your life

→ Not taking the time to research, simply thinking, "these jobs look cool and can make me a lot of money!"

Imagine a year from now and you still have no idea what interest you want to focus on and you're losing sleep over which one seems like the best fit. Take your thoughts and put them on paper. This will help focus on the job that you feel is the best fit at this time in your life. If the job doesn't work out then at least you can refer back to this and find out what you want to do next. After I found out I didn't want to be in the broadcasting industry, I felt lost with no idea what I was going to focus on next. It was one of the worst feelings I have ever experienced.

Action Step:

Pull out a piece of paper and start by writing your name at the bottom and four of your interests.

Once you are finished this step, take the time to pat yourself on the back. Doesn't it feel like a huge amount of pressure has been taken off your shoulders? You took what's in your mind and put it on paper. Now, you can see all of your avenues and you can choose to focus on the one that leaps off the page. I wish I had learned this back in high school. I did this all in my mind and it was hard to focus on the task at hand when all I could think about was if this or that was the right path.

The Uneasy Man

I hope you're finding tons of value in the first three chapters! The next chapter is when we start thinking about the year ahead and I'll teach you an easy way to write down goals that won't seem like a boring task you might have done at school. I like to challenge myself and I like to cross goals off as I complete them. Are you ready to make this the greatest year of your life? If yes, let's get to the next chapter!

4. Create Goals With Milestones

"If you have a goal, write it down. If you do not write it down, you do not have a goal - you have a wish."
- Unknown

Have you ever wanted to learn how to properly write down your goals?

Have you ever felt like you could get more done if you made goal-setting a challenge for yourself?

Have you ever written down goals on a piece of paper and forgot where you put it?

I always thought writing down goals was pointless if I had them in my mind, but I couldn't have been more wrong.

When I finally discovered personal development, I started to come across more and more books that talked about the power of goal setting. All of these authors would say it's important to write down goals because otherwise you'll forget them if you just have them in your mind.

Why don't they teach us this stuff in school? Imagine how beneficial learning how to set up and write down goals would be. Man, I would have got a lot more down if I did this rather than just thinking about goals and doodling in my notebooks to cure boredom.

The Uneasy Man

Now, I was in my early 20's and I never wrote down one goal. This wasn't an easy habit to just pick up.

I wanted to begin writing down my goals, but I had no idea where to begin! There are so many rules that it can actually be very intimidating when it comes to goal writing. I dare you type 'how to set goals' into Google. Watch how many things come up!

I tried a bunch of different methods that I have scattered in several journals around my house, but I couldn't find a method that motivated me to cross my goals off.

Today, If I open up my wallet, I will see a piece of paper that has my goals written out for the year. This was a very tough task at first because It feels weird to write down these goals you want to accomplish for the year. In the beginning, we are groomed to be realistic, go to school, get a job and raise a family.

I took a hard look at what I wanted to complete this year and started writing down the goals that I wanted to achieve on a piece of paper and I posted it on my wall. The first time I did this, I failed miserably. I wrote out my goals on a white board. I still catch a glimpse of the goals I wrote out because I still haven't erased them. I laugh everytime I look at those goals because I didn't complete one! I just wrote them down thinking that was good enough. The good thing is, you don't have to wait for the year to end to start again. It just happened that this year I was writing out new goals in January of 2017, but you can do it anytime. These aren't New Year's Resolutions - we're actually going to do these!

I took out a piece of paper and began writing down my goals for the year. I wrote down things like: 'pay off my visa,' 'publish this book,' 'record an EP,' 'visit Nashville,' 'Live In Australia,' and a couple more. I felt really good about these goals and I folded the piece of paper and stuck it in my wallet.

Many people see writing down your goals as a pointless exercise. They say, "I have my goals in my head." The way I see it, if you can take the goals from your mind and put them on a piece of paper then you are making a commitment to yourself.

Many people feel like they're floating through life because they don't have any goals that they are striving towards. The way I see it, if you have an idea of the goals you want to complete this year than you will be reminded of what was important to you at the start of the year.

Many people think you have to wait to start writing down your goals at the beginning of the year. The way I see it, you can start your yearly goals whenever you would like. The day your pen hits the paper is the start of your new year!

Here are the steps YOU can take to get these results:

Grab a sheet of paper and write out "Goals For The Year" and the date today:

The Uneasy Man

This will remind you of the day that you wrote down these goals. Then count exactly one year from that date for your deadline. A deadline is important because you have to create a sense of urgency, as if these goals must be done by next year.

Number your page from 1 to 10 as big as you can:

you want to take up the full page so you can read this clearly when you awake in the morning. Also writing down these 10 numbers will remind you that you MUST get 10! This could take some time for some people, but keep working on it until you can come up with 10 solid goals that you want to complete this year.

Start each sentence with "I will":

This shows that you are making a promise to yourself that you WILL complete this goal. Commit and do it.

Be specific:

This step is crucial because you have to be able to envision the goal you are creating. Do not say, for example, "I want to lose weight." That's not helping anyone. How much weight do you want to lose? How will you succeed in completing that goal?

Fold this piece of paper and stick it in your wallet and keep it with you at ALL times.

Now, that you have your goals written down on a piece of paper, It's time to choose your number one goal. Which one will you cross off first?

You see, if you just have your goals written out, you will know what you have to do, but that's not good enough. We need to focus on one goal at a time and straight up CRUSH them, but how?

Here's the secret sauce. Take out a piece of paper and write down the goal you want to focus on at the top of the page.

Now, write down every single thing you have to do to achieve that goal. If your goal is "get a job in my field," then write down everything that must be done for you to get that job. You will have to build a resume, improve your LinkedIn, network, search Indeed, put out 10 resumes, get a new suit, etc.. Once you have that done, it's time to go back through these action items and put them in order of importance. You will use a letter system adopted from Brian Tracy's *Eat That Frog.*

Put down the letter 'A' beside everything that has to be done first, then put a 'B' beside everything that has to be done second, 'C' for third and 'D' for last. Here's the final step. When making your list on action steps you will complete, you CANNOT do any B's, C's or D's until all of the 'A's' are complete. No C's without finishing B's and so on!

That is how to CRUSH your goals!

The Uneasy Man

Be sure to avoid these common mistakes:

→ Thinking that goal setting is not important for you.

→ Thinking that you can simply *think* of your goals in your head and that will be good enough.

→ Starting this exercise and not finishing. Isn't that why you aren't where you want to be, because you haven't commited to finishing things? If you stop halfway and say that's good for now, you're setting yourself up for failure!

Imagine you let a year pass by and you didn't write down any goals. How will you know how your year has gone?

Sure, you made some money but did your life improve?

How many more years can you continue to go like this before you break down and have a midlife crisis because you haven't done all the things you wanted to do in your life?

Your biggest regrets in life will not be the things you did, they'll be the things you didn't do.

Action Step:

Begin writing down your 10 goals for the year. You will love this exercise.

Now, that we have that exercise out of our way, I'm sure you feel new fire building in your stomach! There is nothing like writing down goals because the only you want to do is cross that first one off!

Now, that you have the goals you will complete this year, it's important to understand that roadblocks will appear that will try and stop you from completing these goals. We must overcome those obstacles to get closer to our vision. The next chapter will help you uncover some of the fears that are holding you back and how you can finally put them behind you. Go forward, if you dare!

5. Isolate Your Fears

Our fears are like dragons guarding our deepest treasures.
– Rainer Maria Rilke

Have you ever had a fear stop you in your tracks?

Have you ever been so scared of failing that it stopped you from taking a risk?

Have you ever been out with friends and saw an attractive girl or guy and couldn't muster up the courage to simply say "hello?"

I've been there.

When I was 23, I moved to Montreal to start a new life. I had just walked away from my first crack at entrepreneurship and it left a sour taste in my mouth.

I was a part of a clothing brand in my hometown called *Motive*. We wanted to create a clothing company that would inspire young adults to chase their wildest dreams. I met the founder, Cal, after high school. He was a year younger than me and we had never spoken before. We worked out at the same gym in our hometown. While everybody was off at school there weren't too many people living back in town, so we started seeing more and more of each other and developed a great friendship.

33

Cal and I shared this nasty habit of chewing tobacco, which was one of the reasons that brought us together in the first place. Every day after the gym, we would sit in the parking lot and 'toss in a chew' and talk about life. We would talk about how we weren't happy with our lives, what we would rather be doing. We talked about our dreams and how we wanted to start something we could be proud of.

After my epiphany, I wanted to get involved with the world of personal development and I told Cal that I wanted to be a professional speaker. I had no idea what I would talk about. All I knew was I wanted to be on a stage. Cal wanted to create his own company; his dad was an entrepreneur and he knew that was the life for him. At the time, Cal was running a lighting company with his brother. He would purchase lighting kits from China and sell them online and in our hometown. As the weeks went on, Cal started opening up to a new idea that revealed itself. It was a clothing company. I thought owning a clothing clothing company would be the coolest thing, so I told him that I would love to get involved with it.

Our friendship turned into partnership. We spent every day talking about this new brand. We had no direction, all we had was a vision, but that was even a bit blurry. We knew Cal would take care of the business development and I was in charge of the marketing and video content. We began ordering shirts with our logo on it and selling it to friends in our town. We began to make a small name for ourselves. We were the "Motive guys." We tried planning events in the area, but none of them came together because we had no idea what we wanted to concentrate on. Cal and I wanted to take this brand down to the states. We wanted to live in California and come back to Canada in the summer.

I mentioned to Cal that we should drive down to California and promote the brand down there. Cal wasn't crazy about the idea at first, but it grew on him. We chose June 2nd, 2002 as our departure date. We had about four months to plan. We made a post on Facebook and we started raising money for our trip. We wanted to have a going-away party in our hometown and raise funds. We thought it be cool to film a documentary of the trip so we could show our friends and family highlights of our journey. This was before Snapchat and Instagram were huge. I managed to hire a videographer to drive down to Cali with us. I found him on a job posting website called Kijiji. The last sentence of his job posting was, "I am a very spontaneous guy." So, I called him and the first question out of my mouth was, "how spontaneous are you?" He said, "Umm, I'm pretty spontaneous. Why?" I told him that we were looking to hire a videographer to come to California and film a documentary about it. He said "okay, woah, sounds like an awesome idea." I told him about the brand we were creating and he told me that he couldn't make a decision right now, but he would get back to me in a couple days. He got back to me a couple days later and told me that he was interested but we should shoot a video before so we would know what kind of work he did. I told him that was a great idea, and we would do a small video shoot.

I joined the company when I was 21. This was a couple months after my crash. Entrepreneurship wasn't even on my radar at this time, I still wanted to get paid right away for my work, which was the wrong attitude to go into a new project with. We began working on this company everyday. We made a little office at Cal's parents and we spent the days working on the brand and the nights at our part time jobs. I was serving at a burger joint and Cal was working at a hockey rink. Pretty Canadian, eh?

We thought we had a firm grasp on the whole "entrepreneur thing." We had this crazy idea to drive to California and promote the brand. We quit our jobs, hired a videographer and began driving across North America.. The documentary would be about two Canadian guys building their clothing brand and chasing their dreams.

We didn't have one argument before the trip. We knew this trip would be our true test. Spending every waking moment together can be very tough, especially when you have never had any problems previously. Over time, we started to bicker about stupid things that began to drive us apart. It was only a matter of time until we were face to face in a parking lot in the middle of California wanting to fight each other. Adrian, our videographer broke up the argument and told us how stupid we looked. We became fed up with each other and we knew things were never going to go back to the way they were. We realized that our visions for the company were completely different and that we should just part ways and do our own thing.

I walked away from the company that day. Adrian flew home early and it was just Cal and I in California. We weren't talking and I knew it was going to be an awkward drive home. At one point, I wanted to stay in California and make him drive home alone. Luckily, my mother talked some sense into me and told me that I had to drive home with Cal.

The first half of the drive was very quiet. There was no talking. We finally began talking a bit more as the trip proceeded, but we both knew we were done working together on this brand. It was time to move on.

When we got home, we stopped talking to each other completely and we went our separate ways. I didn't want to be in Waterdown anymore. I was tired of answering questions on why *Motive* broke up. I began looking for jobs in different cities and I managed to get hired in Banff, but I didn't take it because I wanted to try living in a city.

When Motive was in full swing, we connected with a guy from Montreal named Scott. He found our company and he loved what we were doing. We began to connect with Scott on a regular basis. After I got home from California, Scott and I jumped on a phone call and I told him all about the trip and how I wanted to move to a new city.

He told me that I should visit him in Montreal and we could talk business. I had never met this guy in my life and here I was thinking about taking a six hour train ride to meet him. I needed a break anyways, so I agreed to meet him in Montreal.

I booked the trip and boarded the train to Montreal. I had a fear of the unknown. I couldn't believe I was travelling to Montreal to have a business meeting with this guy that I had never met. This was WAY out of my comfort zone.

I arrived in Montreal six hours later and Scott met me outside the train station. We drove to a coffee shop to get to know each other. Scott began to tell me about his life and that he was involved with a gym in Montreal where they sold nutritional products and ran bootcamps. I had never heard of a concept like this and I was intrigued to see what this was all about. Scott and I drove over to the gym right smack in the middle of downtown Montreal.

We hopped in an elevator and it took us a couple floors up to a large room that was filled with natural light. The walls were painted white and lime green and there were a bunch of people in workout attire. I remember everyone was so positive and friendly. We sat down at a table and he began to talk about the gym and the products that they sold.

The company was called *Herbalife*. I had never heard of it. I was given a chocolate protein shake and I loved it. I wanted to know more about this company and how I could get involved. I wanted to start a new a project that would take my mind off of *Motive*.

My weekend in Montreal was amazing. I managed to reconnect with an old friend from college who was in montreal working for a TV Production company. He was staying at a fancy hotel downtown and told me I could rent a cot and sleep in his room. The first night, Scott and I went out to grab some beers on the town. On the second night, I went out with some people from the gym and they took me to this incredible karaoke bar that was really busy. I went up and sang some country music.

At the end of the trip, my new friends asked me if I was going to move to Montreal. It didn't cross my mind until they said that. I thought I had to speak French to live there, but they convinced me that I didn't need a second language.

On my way home from Montreal I began thinking about just packing my things and moving back to get involved with that gym and be around positive people.

When I got home, things didn't change. Cal and I still weren't talking. I had to leave. I had such a blast in Montreal that I decided that was the city for me.

I gave myself a two month goal and I saved up as much money as I could at the burger joint. I booked my train, packed all my clothes up, grabbed my guitar and I took off to a new city.

Was I scared? Hell yes, but I was so excited to explore this new city. I knew there were going to be challenges but I was going to face them head on.

Many people could never just get up and move to a new city because of their fear of the unknown. The way I see it is that being scared of something means that you have do it that much more.

Many people need to have the all their ducks lined up before they move away. The way I see it, if it's meant to be, you will find your way. You don't have the see the full staircase, just the first step.

Many people have so many fears that they convince themselves that they are currently happy with their life. The way I see it, people are just so scared to take a chance that they convince themselves that they're happy.

Here are the steps YOU can take to get these results:

Acknowledge your fear:

This is a huge first step. If you just do this today, you've done something great. Many of us have these fears, but they are at the back of our mind, unnoticed, unacknowledged. We try to ignore them and pretend they're not there, but they are. They affect us; every day; all our lives. So acknowledge the fears.

Write it down:

What is your fear? Write it on a piece of paper. Writing it down not only acknowledges that you have it — bringing it out into the light — but it takes away it's power. It takes the fear from the dark, lurking places in the back of your mind, where it has power over you, out into the light of day, outside of you where you have power over the fear. Take control over it by writing it down. It is now outside you. You can do something about it. I personally like to crumple it up and stomp on it, but you can do whatever you like. Post it on your fridge as a reminder of your enemy.

Feel the fear:

You've acknowledged it, but you're still afraid of it. You're reluctant to even have this fear, perhaps even embarrassed about it. Well, no more. Recognize that you're not alone; that we ALL have these fears; that we all think we might not be good enough. Yes, even the amazing Barack Obama, the amazing Jessica Alba, and the amazing Al Pacino. They have the same fears as you do. **Repeat after me: there's nothing wrong with having this fear.** Now allow yourself to feel it. Experience it fully. Bask in this fear. It won't be as bad as you think.

Ask yourself:
- ➔ How serious of a threat is this fear on a scale from 1 to 10?
- ➔ What's the worst thing that could possibly happen?
- ➔ How likely is it to happen?
- ➔ What could you do this week to prevent yourself from having the worst thing happen?

Often the fear isn't that bad after you answer these questions.

Do you fear failing a new career, a new business or a new relationship? What would happen if you did? You'd get another job. You'd move on and you'd live. Do you fear being rejected by someone of the opposite sex? What would happen if you were? You'd lick your wounds, you'd find someone else who is more suited for you and you'd live. Do you fear being broke?

What would happen if you were? You'd cut back on your expenses, perhaps ask family or friends to help you out for a little bit. You'd find a way to make money and you'd live.

These questions will help isolate the fear and desensitize it. You will realize how stupid this fear is once you start to isolate it.

Be sure to avoid these common mistakes:

➔ Allowing fear to hold you back.
➔ Thinking too much and not taking action.
➔ Standing at the edge and never actually jumping!

Imagine that you let the fears holding you back control you for another year or so. What will have to happen for you to finally conquer these fears once and for all? Don't allow yourself to be controlled by these fears anymore. You deserve better!

Action Step:

Isolate the #1 fear that is holding you back. Is it; fear of failure, fear of rejection, fear of loneliness, fear of being judged, fear of death, fear of not living up to your potential? Write it down!

Now that you have isolated your biggest fear, start answering those questions above and desensitize that little bitch, so you can move forward with your life.

The Uneasy Man

In the next chapter, we will start building your foundation. We are going to build your confidence from the ground floor. I will talk to you about the best investment I ever made in my life. I will never regret the time and the money that I invested into **MYSELF.**

Let's learn how to invest in ourselves!

6.Invest Into Yourself

"Investing in yourself is the best investment you will ever make. It will not only improve your life, it will improve the lives of all those around you."

- Robin Sharma.

Have you ever heard the term "invest into yourself" but had no idea what the hell that meant?

Have you ever wanted to start reading personal growth books, but didn't know where to start?

Have you ever felt stagnant in your life and felt you needed to "shake things up?"

Same here - The best thing I could have ever done for myself was beginning to invest into my future self.

After my crash, I took a good look at my life and I knew I had to change somethings. There was this looming fear that would come over me because I had no idea what I would do next and the hardest part was I felt like I couldn't turn to anyone to guide me. Everyone talks about having one mentor that helps guide them through life's obstacles. I didn't have that.

The Uneasy Man

Since I had no car to drive to my internship, I had to take a bus or a train. On the first week back after the crash, my mom offered to drive me to the city where my boss lived and he would come pick me up and drive me in.

My mom left early for work, so I had some time to kill before my boss came. I walked into *Starbucks* to grab a cup of coffee. I paid for my coffee and then I walked over to a seat by the window. I remember looking out the window into the parking lot and thinking, "I have done way too much thinking, I can't do this right now." I needed to do something else. I decided to walk to the bookstore which was connected to the coffee shop.

I began to walk through aisles and browse the books. I wasn't looking for anything in particular, I was just wasting time. I was never much of a reader growing up and the only way I was ever in a bookstore before that day was if I had to write an english essay about a book that I hadn't read. I would go to the bookstore and pick up a *Coles Notes* book and it would summarize the book for me and then I would go home and bullshit an essay about it.

At first, I walked through the fiction section and nothing caught my eye. I found myself in a section that I have never been before. It was called "Self-Help." I didn't have the slightest clue of what these books we're all about. No one ever gave me a book like *Rich Dad, Poor Dad* growing up and said read this. I had to find this out for myself. I began looking through the titles of these books and there was this one that jumped out at me. The book was titled *Stop Worrying & Start Living* by Dale Carnegie. I picked up the book and read the back to see what it was about. This book was talking about the thoughts that were going through my head at this moment of my life. I knew I needed to buy this book, so I took it the front counter to pay for it.

I tried my best to keep busy at work, but I was very excited to get on the train home and read this book. I felt this was exactly what I needed in my life.

Finally it was time to go home. I ran out of the office to catch a bus to the train station. When I finally got on the train, I walked up to the top row, sat down at the window and threw open the book. I managed to get halfway through the book on the train and I finished it later that night in my bed. This book had so much insight into what to do when you are worrying about your future. I knew I had an anxious mind that was very hard to shut off. I believed these thoughts were normal for a man my age who was trying to figure out his life, which they were!

This book taught me about patience, letting life take its course and concentrating on your strengths. I felt I learned so much about myself after reading one book that I was excited to see what else these self help books could do for me. The book reignited my interest in reading and it developed my passion for personal growth. I felt there was so much to learn from these books that I had to start investing my money into buying more.

I went to the bookstore in my hometown and starting picking up more books that interested me. I bought books from Dale Carnegie, Tim Ferris and Jack Canfield. All I wanted to do was read. These books give you tons of exercises that you can do on your own time to help you plan out your future. I started filling up journals of notes, exercises and ideas. I was turning into a totally new person that just wanted to read and implement all of the lessons into my life.

As the time went on, I started learning more, and yes, these books really highlighted some areas I had to work on, but I just kept going. After the books were introduced, I started looking into seminars and conferences from the authors I was reading. I was able to see Tony Robbins speak at a conference in Toronto in 2013. It wasn't his own seminar so it didn't cost thousands of dollars to go.

When I was living in Montreal, I was working a sales job, which I will talk about later. The guy who sat next to me was named Alex. He was a huge fan of Tony Robbins. We would always talk about the books we had read at breaks. We started to become better friends and he told me about a seminar that was coming to Montreal called *Millionaire Mind Experience*. He explained what it was all about and after he told me it was free to attend, I told him I'd go.

The course spread across an entire weekend. I booked the Friday off to attend. The weekend finally arrived and I was starting to get less interested in the course because I worked hard at this sales job and I wanted the weekends to relax and go out with friends. Thursday night came around and a couple friends from the office wanted to grab some drinks.

I still wanted to go the course, so I told myself that I would go out for a couple drinks and then get home so I could sleep. That never happens. The course started at 8:00 in the morning and I was still enjoying myself at 2:00 am. I was having such a good time that I decided I was just going to bail on this course because I didn't *need* it. I finally got in the door at about 3:00 am and didn't set an alarm to wake up for the following morning. I rested my head on the pillow and my eyes opened four hours later without even setting an alarm. I sat up to check the time on my cellphone at it was 7:00 am. A couple seconds later, I received a text from Alex that read "Morning bro, see you amongst the millionaires." I couldn't believe what just happened. I woke up for a reason. I had to go to this course. I managed to shower and get out the door by 7:30!

This course ended up being one of the most amazing things I have ever done and it gave me tons of answers about my life and I even had a couple breakthroughs. By the end, I was in tears because I felt I had more clarity on my life. I met some incredible people that weekend that I still stay in touch with.

By the end of the weekend, I felt like I was a new man. I didn't want this feeling to end. I wanted to continue this journey I was on, so I did something that I didn't think was possible. I bought a course for just under $10,000. I did not have that kind of money, but I felt I was going to learn so much that I could pay it back one day. I definitely wouldn't suggest spending that kind of money if you don't have it, but I was tired of waiting for my life to change. I had to take action. I learned a lot of amazing things from that course and I finally have it all paid off...four years later!

The Uneasy Man

Today I am 26 years old and in the last 5 years I have read a bunch of different books, attended seminars, overcame fears, moved to new cities and now I live in the Grand Cayman Islands. This was all done in the name of "investing into myself." I've been soaking up all the information I could for the last five years and this book is what I have learned.

Many people will have a million excuses on why they shouldn't invest in themselves. Some people invest into houses, I invest into myself. The way I see it, investing in yourself is only going to make you stronger which will lead to making more money in the future.

Many people just have never heard of that term - investing into yourself - and if they have they quickly say that's not for me. The way I see it, people CHOOSE not to hear "invest into yourself."

Many people want to start investing in themselves but find it overwhelming. The way I see it is there are thousands of books. Find the first book that attracts you and read it then move on. Don't overthink it.

Here are the steps YOU can take to get these results:

Find a topic that resonates with you:

The first step in investing into yourself is finding knowledge on the topic that you feel is your biggest challenge. You see, my biggest challenge was worry and when I found a book that had worrying in the title, it was a no brainer.

What is biggest challenge in your life right now that you want to overcome?

Do you want to learn how to save money? Invest into real estate? Become more confident in a social setting? Learn entrepreneurship, online marketing, sales or overcome your worry and anxiety? If it's the last one then you are reading the right book (wink).

Think about the one thing that keeps coming up in your head and begin learning about it. The more knowledge you have on the the subject, the easier it will be to overcome that challenge,

Take your time on the book:

When I was first starting out, I thought I had to read as many books as fast as I possibly could. Rushing through books is not a good way to retain information. You want to read each chapter with a highlighter or a pen. I want you to read through this book slowly and highlight parts that you find interesting.

If you think spending hundreds or even thousands of dollars on books, products, and seminars will change you, you are wrong. I thought that if I invested this money that I would follow this easy road to making my money back. Implementing the things you have learned is the real tip for success.

The Uneasy Man

I want you to invest your hard earned money in these products because they won't buy themselves but, once you have them, no will tell you when to read them or when to do the homework. You are 100% responsible for your actions and nothing will come from it if you don't invest your most precious resource: your time.

Be sure to avoid these common mistakes:

→ Thinking that you don't need to invest into yourself.
→ Overthinking the first book you want to read.
→ Spending thousands of dollars on a course that you don't have money for. Yes I did this and it wasn't fun paying it back for three years of my life. It stopped me from doing a lot of things.

Invest into yourself every chance you can.

Once you start, you won't want to stop.

Imagine you let a year go by and you still haven't began investing into yourself. Maybe you do some stuff here and there, but you haven't really begun. Imagine how many books you could have read or things you could have learned. The two best times to plant a tree are: twenty years ago and today.

Action Step:

Go to *Amazon* and type in the topic you want to learn about. Find a book that has a high star rating and tons of great reviews. Start there or go to your local bookstore and walk through the self help section and buy the first book that jumps out at you.

Once you have done that, take the time to read the book thoroughly and take in as much as you possibly can. Highlight parts, write notes, write out your ideas and move on once you have a firm grasp of the book.

These are the kind of things that will build your confidence. Investing in yourself is crucial in getting that, but the next chapter is when we will start learning about something every successful person does in the morning. There is something that ALL successful people have in common and you will find out what that is in the next chapter!

7. Craft A KIller Morning Routine

"When you arise in the morning, think of what a precious privilege it is to be alive—to breathe, to think, to enjoy, to love— then make that day count!"
- Steve Maraboli, *Life, the Truth, and Being Free*

Have you heard that the most famous people in the world do the same thing every morning?

Have you ever wanted to create a routine that you could do every morning that put you into a great state of mind and body?

Have you ever started a routine and then as soon as saturday rolled around you stopped and said, "I'll start back up on Monday" Then Monday came around you didn't feel like it?

I was in the same boat!

I always tried creating the most complex morning routines when all I needed was something simple that I could do everyday.

Mornings have always been very hard for me. I always had trouble waking up and starting my day, mostly because I wouldn't sleep much at night. I would usually toss and turn all night thinking about my life and then finally get to sleep early in the morning.

However, when you have nobody making your schedule, you have to motivate yourself to rise out of bed. I always just got up and went straight to the coffee machine. That was my excitement for the morning. I started hearing about the power of morning routines. Every book I read, the author was talking about these morning routines and how much it changed their lives. I started looking into these routines and I wanted to create one but had no idea where to start. If you are in that position right now, stick around and I'll talk about it!

I have tried different routines before, but the one I felt would work best had to be simple and something I could do everyday. If it is too long, you won't be motivated to do it after a night of drinking or staying up late. So make this as simple and effective as possible.

I started tinkering with a couple routines and I found one that works great for me. I wake up every morning and chug a bottle or glass of water as fast as possible to give my body a shock. Next, I will grab my shoes and go for a 15-20 minute walk or run and do some pushups and burpees. Once I get home, I have a cold shower and then start brewing a cup of coffee. After I get my coffee, I do my self-confidence exercises, read, plan my day then meditate for ten minutes.

Many people don't see the importance of a morning routine because they get up too late and don't have time before work. The way I see it is, imagine how much more focused you could be if you took 30 minutes for yourself every morning and got mentally and physically ready for the day.

Many people will want to create this morning routine for Monday to Friday, but skip the weekends. The way I see it is to start seeing the results, you MUST do it 7 days a week. No excuses.

Many people see waking up, drinking a coffee, showering and grabbing a banana on their way out the door as a good enough morning routine. The way I see it is your mornings should be a time for you to set yourself up for the day. I can't stand the feeling of being rushed.

Here are the steps YOU can take to get these results:

Make a list:

The first step is to gather information on what you need to get done daily. Make a list of seven or eight things you would like to get done. Start with making a commitment on the time you will wake up every morning. Next, what is the first thing you do when you spring out of bed? Feel free to copy mine or make your own.

Sculpt the flow:

Now that you are done your first draft, it's time to organize the flow of things. Picture yourself running through your routine. Move items up and down until you feel they are in the right spot.

If seven or eight is too many. Start with three.

When I was first starting out, I picked

1. Drink A Large Glass of Water
2. Go For A Walk
3. Daily Gratitude

Feel free to start small if you ever never tried to do a morning routine. You can always add things to your list as time goes on. After some time, you will want to do more. It's nice to keep it fresh.

My morning routine is much stronger now and it looks like this:

Wake up @ 7 AM - No Snooze
Large Glass of Lemon Water
Walk + Exercise (30 mins)
Cold Shower
Coffee
Plan Out My Day
Read 15-20 Minutes
Self-Confidence Exercises
Meditate
Gratitude

Now that is a KILLER morning routine, wouldn't you say?

Test Drive

Take your new routine for a spin and see how it feels for the first couple of days. When you are done your routine, ask yourself how you feel? Is there something you're missing? If so, try and find the missing piece. I want you to feel like you can take on the day after you do these things.

Be sure to avoid these common mistakes:

- → Not being specific and just saying, "wake up early"
- → Not doing your routine on weekends.
- → Not giving yourself enough time to get the routine down before you have to leave.
- →

Morning routines are a powerful tool that you can use if you are self employed or employed by someone else. We all have things to do each day that can advance our business or advance our job. If we just go into the day without the right mindset, we will feel like our day was 'busy' rather than 'productive.'

Imagine a year from now, you still haven't created a solid morning routine and you wonder why your business or your job isn't where you want it to be. It's probably because you just did whatever came to mind rather than focusing on what needs to be done for the day.

Action Step:

Take action right now and create your first draft. Be specific and add as many items as your heart desires. Just remember. You will be doing this **EVERY** morning.

There you have it, your routine has a creative process. Now, it's time to take your routine to the next level by introducing mindfulness into your practice!

Let's go!

8. Create Mindfulness

"If you want to conquer the anxiety of life, live in the moment, live in the breath."
- Amit Ray, Om Chanting and Meditation

Have you ever wanted to meditate but you couldn't sit still?

Have you ever wanted to do yoga, but felt it was only for women?

Have you ever thought that going to the gym is the only form of exercise you need?

I used to believe that too, but I have learned that yoga and meditation are my new favourite things, and this is coming from an ex gym rat.

Like many people in the world today, I have had my struggles with anxiety and worry and to be honest I have always kept it to myself. Sharing your story on Facebook and getting likes and comments is not going to help you with it. You must take care of it before you start to share your story. That's what I believe at least. I have been battling with my mind since I was in high school.

In October of 2016, I finally said enough is enough. I was $4000 in credit card debt, $1500 in overdraft so I couldn't even use my debit card, $800 cell phone bill, no cellphone, no job and I was just about to have a hernia surgery done. My anxiety was at an all time high and all I would do is sit on the couch, drink coffee and watch netflix. I knew I was feeling this way because of all the things that weren't going right in my life but I didn't know how to shake it and move forward. This was probably one of the worst times next to the days following my car crash.

I remember sitting on my deck with a cigarette in my mouth and thinking, "what the fuck am I doing? I am way better than this!" I grabbed my jacket and walked myself into the doctor's office to talk about what was going on in my mind.

My self-doubt was so bad that negative thoughts would just fill my head all day.

As I waited in the doctor's office, I felt relieved to finally be asking for help because that was one thing I hated to do. I felt I could take on life by myself, but I quickly learned that no man is an island. We all need help once in awhile.

As I sat with the doctor, explaining what was going on in my head, the doctor sat across from me, listening and asking questions. He asked me things like "how long has this been going on?" I told him a long time, but it's never been this bad. He said there was a good chance I had an anxiety disorder and prescribed some medication to me. I was interested in taking anything that would help these thoughts disappear.

I received the prescription and walked out of the door with a small sense of relief. I popped my first pill and he told me to take the pills for two weeks and then return for a follow-up. I started taking the pills and, for the first five days, I felt they helped a bit and made me calm down. But then my mind started to act up again and I felt I was taking the easy way out, so I stopped taking them. I didn't even go for the follow up meeting.

The Uneasy Man

I left it for a couple weeks, which was the wrong thing to do because the heavy anxiety picked up again. I went back to the doctor and apologized for not showing up for the follow up. I told him I wasn't doing good, but I wanted to find out what was wrong with me and I didn't want any medication until I knew. He told me he was going to book a meeting with psychiatrist to talk about some things and that he would examine me and tell me what he thought was going on.

By the time I went to the psychiatrist, I had a job serving and bartending at a restaurant, I quit smoking and I was fully recovered from my surgery. I was in a much better state, but I still wanted to see what the doctor had to say.

We sat down for about an hour, talking all about my life and all the things that had happened so he could understand where I was coming from. He finally said that he could see that anxiety is definitely there, but also that I have an artistic mind. He told me he wanted to try a new medication that will either help me or make me feel worse. He said I would only have to take it for three weeks until we could find a proper diagnosis. Again, I took these pills for about a week and then I gave up on them again because they made me feel groggy and not myself. I went back into his office and told him that I didn't want medication. I wanted to find out how to overcome my anxiety the natural way and he said that was possible too.

He gave me a couple resources to investigate. One of them was a book was called *The 10 Best Anxiety Techniques Ever*. I ordered the book from Amazon and started reading it. The book gave me some ideas on how to help panic attacks and anxiety. The biggest thing was diaphragm breathing. The second book he gave me was *ADHD For Adults*.

I went back to my doctor three weeks later and told him that I stopped taking the drugs. I couldn't do it. I knew overcoming my anxiety naturally would be more challenging, but I was committed to finding a way.

There was an all-natural stress reliever the doctor knew of and he said it might work - St. John's Wort. I bought some and began taking a pill every morning. I used those pills for a good length of time. Today, I don't take any medication. I live in the Cayman Islands where it's sunny everyday and the beaches are breathtaking. I exercise, meditate and try new things. I have a clarity in my life. My anxiety doesn't speak up anymore and it's one of the greatest feelings. I know I am on my way.

The first time I heard about mindfulness was when I was living in Montreal. I had a friend that went to a meditation class once a week and asked me if I wanted to go. This would have been something that I would never have done if I was living in my hometown. Since I wasn't living in my hometown, I felt it easier to explore different interests.

I walked into this old building, up a flight of stairs to this room where there was a bunch of people sitting cross legged on the floor. We found a little spot at the back of the room and we sat there listening to the this guy play some kind of instrument that I had never seen before at the front of the room. I couldn't understand what he was saying because he was speaking in French, so I just listened to the music and did what I could. I listened to my breath and tried to stop the chatter in my mind. I tried meditation by myself before this and I felt so bored sitting there that I finally gave up. Luckily, the music helped to ease my mind and allowed me to concentrate on my breath.

After that class, I began to read more about meditation, I wanted to practice at home so I scoured the internet looking for a method to do so and I came across some cool methods to try. I made it my goal to create a habit of doing meditation more often. To be honest, it was brutal at first. I always thought I was doing it wrong or it wasn't working, but I quickly learned that there is no right way to meditate.

I enjoy meditation but something that has been even more beneficial for me was yoga. Talk about being uncomfortable! In high school, I was a jock who played sports and now I'm attending hot yoga classes? Man, this was going to be hard to accept. I went to my first hot yoga class in Montreal and loved it, but I still felt so awkward doing it and I knew it was going to take some time before I felt comfortable. I think it was a bit of my social anxiety coming out because I felt like everyone was watching me and laughing at my poses if I couldn't do them right.

Today, I am much more confident about doing yoga and I am happy telling people because it makes me very happy and really eases my anxiety. I've started to get more confident in my poses and that makes me feel better when I'm doing it in public. Everyone learns at their own pace and I found that it was a good idea to start doing home practices until I felt ready for the public yoga.

Many people may feel that yoga is only for women who wear yoga pants, but the way I see it, it's for anyone who wants to connect to their true power and create mindfulness in their life.

Many people think meditation is boring and that it's hard to silence your mind. Putting some movement into it and concentrating on your breathing helps. Meditation doesn't have to be simply sitting still in one place.

Many people are afraid to do yoga because of what other people might think of them but the way I see it, starting yoga at home will get you more comfortable with a couple of the positions and once you learn some yoga slang, you will feel more comfortable in public.

Here are the steps YOU can take to get these results:

Practice at home:

Personally, I found the best way to learn the techniques and have fun with it is watching, "Yoga With Adriene" on YouTube. She makes yoga fun and she can take you from being a newbie to a veteran in about 30 days. She starts of with the fundamentals and by the end you will start to do more advanced positions.

Practice everyday:

"Yoga with Adriene" has a 30 day camp. You can do yoga for 30 days at home and you will feel way more confident after this is done.

Go public with it:

The Uneasy Man

Once you are starting to do all the positions with the really funny names then you are ready for the big leagues. Buy a mat, grab a free pass, and don't get distracted by all the pretty women doing yoga. Practicing yoga is an incredible experience that I highly recommend!

Be sure to avoid these mistakes:

→ Thinking 'mindfulness' is just meditation.
→ Going to public yoga too early, feeling uncomfortable, and never going back.
→ Thinking you can't do yoga because you aren't flexible enough. If the you are doing hot yoga, it is much easier to stretch your muscles.

If you feel like yoga could benefit you and help you ease your anxious mind then it's time to begin doing it and getting better at it. Imagine a couple months go by and you still haven't tried it and you still feel like your days are just rushing by. If you're saying to yourself, "yeah, that sounds about right." Then, my friend, you need to create mindfulness.

Action Step:

Go to YouTube and type in "Yoga With Adriene" if you would like to start easing into yoga. If mediation is what you're after then you can download an app on your phone. I have used "Calm" before and I recently downloaded "Headspace." Both are very good!

Mindfulness will allow you to quiet the voices in your head that keep telling you what to do. Once you begin to master mindfulness, you will feel like your days are much more enjoyable, but you will need to implement the next chapter. This is where we will dive into productivity and how you get tons of work done in a small period of time without feeling exhausted. Sounds like something you'd be interested in? Well, what are you waiting for? Let's go!

9. Hack Your Productivity

"Amateurs sit and wait for inspiration, the rest of us just get up and go to work."
— Stephen King, On Writing: A Memoir of the Craft

Have you ever wanted to *finally* stop using excuses and go after your dream life?

Have you ever woke up in the morning and had so much to do that you instead of getting to work, you just went back to bed?

Have you ever wanted to learn how to create an effective to-do list?

I'm with you there!

Planning out your day can be very challenging sometimes. There would be some days when I would wake up and have no clue what I needed to get done for that day because my thoughts were so scattered. However, there were days when I knew exactly what had to be done.

There comes a time in our lives when you have to admit that you're not happy with where you are and that it's time to make a change that will improve your future. But how?

I have had **TONS** of these moments, but I ended up reverting back to my comfort zone after obstacles arrived, and here's why:

I felt externalized pressure from society that it was too "hard" to be an entrepreneur and I also felt the internalized pressure of trying to prove people wrong.

Coming up with business ideas was not the hard part for me, it was sticking to them.

The biggest thing I want to do is inspire, not just through words but the way I'm living my life. I know that I will never settle for a 'good enough' job that gives me the same paycheque every week. I know that I have always been meant for more and it's about sticking with that long enough until it starts to unfold.

The biggest challenge in that is believing in yourself when the rest of the world doesn't. When times are hard and the world feels like it's against you, it's about swallowing your pride and doing whatever it takes to get the job done.

I've always picked up odd jobs here and there and the one industry that I always enjoyed working in and was good at was serving and bartending. I started in the industry when I was 18 and am still in the industry as I'm writing this book at age 26. I can't wait for the day when I don't have to be behind the bar and I'm entertaining people from a stage.

I always keep where I'm going in my mind, I know these jobs are just a means to an end. Sometimes you have put things on hold to get your life back on track. That was always hard for me to do because I felt like people thought of me as just a 'bartender with hobbies' and that I was going to be doing this for the rest of my life. That's totally fine for some people, but I didn't want to do that.

If you are not where you want to be and you're not waking up with this burning desire to work on yourself then what do you need to change?

Many people see their life as a straight line. Get a job and work your way up. The way I see it is. there is grand vision and the path to get there will look like a lot more like a four-year-old's doodle than a straight line.

I heard a great quote from Mike Babcock, coach of the Toronto Maple Leafs. He said, "make your highs longer than your low's and you will find yourself in a great place at the end."

Many people don't see the benefit of waking up early and starting your day on the right foot. The way I see it is waking up early is a very important ingredient in creating the life of your dreams. I may not be perfect, but I still see the benefits.

Many people think they will never amount to a bigger life because of the limiting beliefs and the thoughts they carry. The way I see it is everyone has the right to create the life of their dreams no matter what anyone says. Some of the most successful people in the world today came from childhoods that we couldn't even imagine and look where they are now. They used their misfortune to fuel themselves. They didn't want that life for their future family.

What's our excuse?

Here are the steps YOU can take to get these results:

Boost your dopamine levels:

Dopamine has been called our "motivation molecule." It boosts our drive, focus and concentration. It enables us to plan ahead and resist impulses so we can achieve our goals. It gives us that "I did it!" lift when we accomplish what we set out to do. Dopamine makes us competitive and provides the thrill of the chase in all aspects of life — business, sports, and love.

Doesn't that sound like something you want?

Here are a couple of my favorite ways to boost my dopamine levels naturally:

Listen to music:

Studies have shown that if you listen to music you really enjoy, the brain releases dopamine as a response. Even the anticipation of hearing that music also increases dopamine levels, which is probably why you see all these crazy lines in front of music stores.

Meditate:

Sometimes the best way to do something is by doing nothing. Specifically, you do nothing physically but in your mind you're trying to sort out your thoughts. Whether you meditate, pray or do simple self-reflection, all these activities are linked to increased dopamine levels.

Establish a streak:

A streak is just a visual reminder of how many consecutive times you achieved something. In games, it's often used to track wins but you can also use it in everyday activities for the added dopamine boost.

The easiest way to do this is to take a calendar and put an X in the box everyday you do something, like cleaning your desk or eating a healthy lunch. Soon enough, you'll have a neat row of X's there to show off your streak.

Having a streak increases dopamine production in the same way completing a task does. While you haven't completed the entire goal, just knowing that you're going in the right direction makes your brain give you enough of a dopamine burst to keep on going.

Cross off your tasks for the day:

Dopamine is also released after you finish something, whether it's a big job or a small task.

As I said above, you need to write down those tasks in a list. It's not that I don't trust you to remember your to-dos, it's just that it's much more satisfying, dopamine-wise, to check stuff off a list physically. Nothing is more satisfying than crossing off something you've done.

Get in the habit of writing down the things you must do the next day before you eat dinner.

Let's say you finish of your to-do list today and instead of closing your computer and going to eat dinner, take the time to write down what you want to do the next day. Everything will be so fresh in your mind because you know everything that needs to be done.

If you are anything like me than you know that if you begin thinking about your to-do list while you're laying in bed there is good chance you will not be getting any sleep, and getting up early in the morning to write out a to-do list doesn't really make me want to 'jump' out of bed either.

I like to warm up my dopamine by starting off with a couple EASY tasks like making my bed or drinking a glass of water. It sounds simple but when you actually physically cross that thing off your list, you become motivated to move on to the next thing and cross that off!

Before you know it, you're at the end of your day and it has been an insanely productive one. There shouldn't be a minimum or maximum amount of things you could do in a day. Just keep going till you physically can't anymore. It all depends on your energy and what you want to prioritize. I like to shoot for two to three major tasks and the other ones are just simply things to either release some dopamine or things I need to remember like 'go to the grocery store and do laundry.'

Dopamine is an addictive chemical but in a good way. It helps motivate you in doing things you need to do, even if you don't want to do them. And have you noticed something? Most of the things I mentioned above are actually activities that also make you more productive, since that's essentially what dopamine does.

I hope you enjoyed this chapter on productivity hacks that you can use to get the most out of your day. Which activities are you already doing and which ones do you want to include in your day. I think everyone should use their dopamine to create effective to-do lists and you could even start a streak with the amount of days that you do this!

Imagine you let a year go by and you still haven't learned how to hack your productivity. How will that make you feel? You will continue to start things and never want to finish. Create competition with yourself because at the end of the day that is our greatest opponent.

Be sure to avoid these common mistakes:

→ Trying to raise your dopamine with over-the-counter drugs. It's better if you do it naturally.
→ Not writing down your list and **CROSSING** them off.
→ Not planning your day the night before.

Action Step:

Decide which activity you will use to boost your dopamine levels. Stop what you are doing and turn on your favorite song, make a to-do list, meditate or exercise. All of these things will release that wonderful natural drug called dopamine and you will open the flood gates to productivity

Now, that you have learned how to spike your dopamine levels, it's time to start learning how to become comfortable in uncomfortable situations. This is very important step in overcoming your anxiety, building confidence and living a life of freedom. Let's get it!

10. Get Comfortable Being Uncomfortable

"True success is achieved by stretching oneself, learning to feel comfortable being uncomfortable."

— Ken Poirot

Have you ever been so scared of something that you couldn't move?

Have you ever said, "that's way too far out of my comfort zone, I won't do it?"

Have you ever felt your anxiety peak when you had to a something you were really scared to do?

AH! Same here. I used to dread being uncomfortable, but now I harness it. If I'm scared to do something, it means It **must** be done.

When I first moved to Montreal, I felt I was confident, but there were so many fears I still had to overcome. I was scared to sing at open mics, I was scared to talk with pretty women, I was scared to cold call people, I was scared to live on my own and fend for myself. As much as I was scared, I knew I had to overcome these things and, one by one, I started becoming more confident and more unstoppable. Breaking through the fears made for some incredibly awkward nights and times when I just wanted to curl up into a ball and die because of the embarrassment. Man, am I glad I had them now. I'm not saying everyone will have the same experience but there's a good chance that you will fail and that's totally OK. The best thing to do is do it with someone just as new as you so you can laugh in the face of failure. Overcoming a fear alone makes you feel isolated. If you're new to this whole becoming uncomfortable thing, find a friend. It will make the experience much more enjoyable.

Today, there are still fears in my life, but when I'm faced with a new challenge, I tell myself that "I'm growing!" Telling myself that makes me take action.

Many people get too comfortable in their comfort zone and never stretch themselves. They just watch people growing and they feel stuck. I see a comfort zone as something that needs to be stretched if you want to live a bigger life.

Many people see something that scares them and say, "I can't do this." Therefore, they never try. The way I see it, the things that scare you are the things you have to do. Do it before your mind kicks in and you start overthinking.

Many people see being uncomfortable as something that will not benefit them in the future. The way I see it, you will notice a relatively fast solution to this if you just take action. It's crazy how much the "uncomfortable muscle" can grow in a matter of days or weeks.

The Uneasy Man

Here are the steps I took to get those results:

Clear your head:

Every time I try something new and different, my inner voice gets really loud. The only way to make it quiet is to clear the noise around and inside me. A little yoga or meditation goes a long way in providing space between thoughts so you can think about something on a deeper level.

Write about the process:

When you are feeling uncomfortable you need to release that tension to move forward. Writing about it is a great way to express the feelings and relieve the pressure. It also helps organize your thoughts and emotions so you can get a clear picture of the path ahead.

Reward yourself:

If you are going to put yourself through a bit of Hell you are certainly entitled to a bit of Heaven as well. Get yourself something nice. Indulge with that once-a-year restaurant. You are taking risks and working hard. Show yourself that **YOU** appreciate **YOU** for making this happen.

Share your journey:

Some challenges are yours and yours alone. But that doesn't mean you have to feel lonely in the process. Include your closest friends or a great coach in the process so they can support you and be entertained by your struggles and eventual success. If you can entice another friend to join you on the journey, it's even better.

Create easy time:

When you are pushing for a breakthrough everything can seem hard. Make sure you set time away for simple tasks that you have mastered previously. This will rebuild your confidence and remind you that you have broken through the difficulty before.

Take the plunge:

Toe dipping into the danger zone makes it hard to really get things going. Being fully immersed in an uncomfortable environment may be more stressful but at least you'll get the whole experience moving forward and become closer to your vision.

Celebrate small wins:

The struggle through growth provides a steady good kind of pain and suffering but it's generally a long process. Set recognizable milestones to the process and get excited every time you reach one. Be proud and pleased with each progressive step you achieve. Then party BIG TIME when you get to the finish line.

The Uneasy Man

Be sure to avoid these common mistakes:

- → Being too scared to stretch your comfort zone.
- → Not acknowledging your fears.
- → Thinking that you don't have to do this to become confident.

Imagine you let that fear go on for another year and every time it comes up, you wash it down with a glass of self-doubt. You will get so scared that it will literally make you hyperventilate. Now, what if you just finally swallowed the fear and took massive action?

No. It won't be easy, **BUT YOU ARE GROWING**!

Action Step:

Find one task that makes you sweat just thinking of it and make a commitment to yourself that you will do it this week. Talk to a good-looking girl or guy, sing in public, skip down the street or try ordering pizza from Mcdonald's. I dare you to do the last one. If you do, film it and send it to me.

Now, so far in this book, we have been working on the mental side. We are going to switch over to some physical things you can do overcome your anxiety, stop your worry and build authentic confidence.

If you are ready, turn the page!

11. Walk Like You Mean It

"Confidence is being able to say 'Fuck you, I'm the shit' without opening your mouth, say it with your walk, with your smile, say it with your entire being."

- Tati-Ana Mercedes

Have you ever seen someone walking down the street and thought, "That person looks so confident. How do I get that?"

Have you ever been walking down the street and wanted the opposite sex to notice you?

Have you ever been told that your walk says *A LOT* about you?

I have!

I've always wanted to display a confident walk. I didn't want people to see me walking around looking at the floor and having my shoulders rolled over. I was always able to come off as a confident person even though I was pretty insecure. I couldn't let people see that. That is why I think people don't believe me when I tell them I have anxiety.

The Uneasy Man

They always say, "no way, you have been confident your whole life."

In high school I wasn't as confident as I am now (what a surprise). High school brings out the insecurity in all of us. We have all felt young and insecure at times, and at other times felt like we had this whole 'life' thing under control. My peers always thought I was confident because of they way I held myself. I would always be thinking about posture while I was walking and standing. I wanted to portray confidence even if I wasn't feeling very confident that particular day.

Did you know there are coaches in the world that teach you how to move? They will teach you how to walk, stand and move so you look and feel more confident. I thought that was amazing. I was fortunate enough to learn from the one of the top movement coaches in the world, Jean-Louis Rodrigue. He has been an acting coach for over 20 years and been teaching the *Alexander Technique.* His unique approach to movement, education, and to improving the levels of performance has brought international recognition.

I was taught the technique in San Diego when I was attending Bo Eason's storytelling seminar. Eason helps you carve out your personal power story and how to get the audience to attach themselves to your every word. Jean-Louis Rodrigue talked to us about releasing our inner animal. At first, I felt way out of comfort zone, but as I looked around the stage I noticed everyone was starting to harness their inner animal and they were taking it seriously. I always felt like I was a lion, so I started to move like one and man, did I ever feel powerful!

What animal do you resemble? Take a second to think about how that animal walks. I'm not going to make you put down this book and walk like that animal unless you **really** want to. I have easier steps that will help you improve your walk and if you feel like incorporating subtle gestures of your animal, be my guest. It's your walk.

Many people think that walking with confidence isn't an important thing to cultivate and that it just comes natural when you are successful. The way I see it, walking with confidence will help you snap out of your rut if you are having an **off** day.

Many people might think you can't improve your walk - it's just genetic! The way I see it, you should try and be aware of your walk so you can give off a good impression before you even open your mouth. Confidence is sexy, you must know that by now.

Many people think someone that walks confident is rich and successful. They way I see it, someone who walks with confidence is comfortable in their own body and even if they aren't rich and successful, they've made you think they were, and sometimes that's half the battle.

Here are the steps I took to get those results:
Walking with confidence is an art:

Start by noticing where you can improve your walk. Are you looking down, arms swinging or walking too fast?

Good posture:

You should be looking straight ahead with your head level and your arms naturally at your side. Walk at a slow, comfortable speed and smile. It doesn't have to be an ear to ear grin; make it subtle.

Stand with a slight bend:

When you are standing, keep a little bend in your knees and ground yourself. Don't lock your knees and stand up straight. That doesn't look as confident as you may think.

Be sure to avoid these common mistakes:

- ➔ Walking too fast
- ➔ Swinging your arms
- ➔ Smiling so much that it looks forced.

You may not think that walking is that important but every time you are are walking around from now on, I bet you will be noticing some things about yourself and trying to improve your walk. Not only will it make people react different, but It will make people react *to you* differently and you will become hooked!

Action Step:

Take action right now and think about something you can improve on with your walk. Try and implement as many of the tips above on your next walk.

12. Network Like A Professional

"When you are networking you are doing more than just marketing your business; you are marketing yourself."

— Timothy M. Houston, *No-Nonsense Networking: The Straightforward Guide to Making Productive, Profitable and Prosperous Contacts and Connections*

Have you ever been at an event and felt like a lost puppy?

Have you ever started talking to someone in your industry but had no idea how to explain what you do?

Have you ever thought you had to be very successful to network with other successful people?

I was in the same boat. Becoming efficient is the secret to becoming a networking master. You want to get as much work done in the least amount of time.

I have always been an upbeat person that enjoyed meeting new people, but if I was alone in a room of strangers, my anxiety would kick in a bit. I never enjoyed networking because I felt it was a room filled with people all talking about what they want to do and how other people can help them get to that point. I was looking at it all wrong. Networking should be about giving, not taking. Give first, receive later. There were some events where I would get into these incredibly awesome conversations that led to a friendship, but there was never any strategy - I felt it was just lucky. I wanted to learn how to become efficient and get the most out of each event that I walked into. I began researching and gaining some valuable information about the networking world and I started to become more confident and excited to go to these events. I managed to write an ebook all about creating first impressions at networking events. You can find it on Amazon under *"How To Create A Killer First Impression In Business."* The book was all about walking into a room and owning it. Meeting new people can help you take your confidence to the next level.

Many people see a networking event as something boring. They way I see it is, if you are going to boring networking events, you're going to the wrong ones. Find ones that feel like a night out.

Many people think networking is about talking to the most amount of people in one night. The way I see it, talking to a couple people and building meaningful connections that blossom outside of the event is the real key.

Many people think creating a connection is talking all about what they do and finding someone that can help them. The way I see it, if you reach out to help someone first, they will be more inclined to help you in the future.

Here are the steps I took to get those results:

Go to more events:

It's that simple. Find more events that interest you and go to them. You can find great events in your town just be looking online. Believe me, they are there!

Act like you want to be there:

When you are at these events, be present. Don't sit in the back of the room on your phone. Focus on what is going on, be involved and smile. This makes it much easier for people to approach you.

Be Interested rather than interesting:

This is the *golden* rule. Instead of talking about yourself and what you do. Be interested in what others do and only tell them what you do when they ask.

Leave people with a lasting impression:

When leaving a conversation. Leave them with something they will remember you by. Have a really flashy business card. That's one way or say, "Hey, we should continue this conversation some other time, take down my number and Facebook name," or exchange business cards. Just so you know, people take a lot of pride in their business cards. They are usually really proud of them. Don't just take it from them and throw it in your pocket. Take a couple seconds to look at it and admire it. It's a small thing, but it goes a long way.

Be careful and avoid these common mistakes:

- → Going to events that don't excite you
- → Being distracted at the events and not being present
- → Talking about yourself and not listening.

Action Step:

Look in your area for upcoming network events that correlate with your interests. You can head to *Meetup* and browse through some events or if you interested in improving your public speaking, find the closest *Toastmaster* meeting and go to it! I swear there is one in every town or city.

Networking is an amazing way to help yourself get to the next level in your business or your life. If you don't learn how to network, you will always be the person walking around the room and just talking to random people and not to the people who will help you grow. Imagine a year goes by and you still haven't attended ONE networking event in your industry. Think about how many amazing people you could have met if you just went!

Now that you have some motivation behind going to these networking events, you need to find a way to convince your friends to go if you aren't interested in going alone. Sure, you may be alone for a bit but I'm sure you can meet someone to strike up a conversation with. If you still **do not** want to go alone, then the next chapter is for you. You will learn how to lead the pack and do the things you want to do. Your friends will enjoy your decision-making skills and they will go along. Trust me.

13. Take Charge Of Decisions

"The greatest leader is not necessarily the one who does the greatest things. He is the one that gets the people to do the greatest things."

— Ronald Reagan

Have you ever felt like you do what only everyone else wants to do?

Have you ever wanted your friends to be excited with where you want to go?

Have you ever wanted to lead the pack rather than follow behind?

You're speaking my language. Growing up, I was very impressionable. I did what everyone else was doing, and I'm glad I'm done with that part of my life.

In high school, lunch time was always the time to socialize. You either ate in the cafeteria or went out to grab lunch. In my school, we had this large atrium where all the so called "popular" kids would hang out. Luckily, since I played hockey, I was included in this group. Senior's ran

90

the atrium, and it was intimidating if you were freshman or a sophomore. You knew walking into the atrium left you open for gawking eyes, rude comments or having something thrown at you. When I finally made it to senior year, my grade ran the atrium and we weren't the ones scared to walk in. We had our years of torture. It was time to bask in the glory.

We had a small plaza close to the school where we could get pizza, Chinese food, chicken wings, etc. and then bring it back to the atrium. Pizza was always the cheapest, but you could only eat so many times in a week. Every now and again, I would say, "Hey guys, let's go somewhere different." My friends weren't interested in changing it up so instead of getting what I wanted, I would just follow along. I know this is a silly example of leading the pack, but I felt this started me down my path of wanting to be a leader and not a follower. I wanted to blaze my own path and have people follow me!

In college, we would drink every weekend at this club called Barracuda. My friends and I would complain how much we disliked this place when we were sober, but we always liked going where everyone else was going. That's normal right? Once in awhile, I tried being the 'voice of reason' but it usually ended up not working and I would find myself drunk on the dancefloor at Barracuda...again.

I started becoming more dominant over time because I started gaining more self-confidence. I was doing the things I wanted to do and learning how to say 'NO' to things I really didn't want to do. It was rare, but the muscle was growing! I feel like I became more convincing after college. Friends began asking me, "where are you going this weekend?" This was usually followed up by: "I'm coming." My guy friends liked going out with me because when I got drinking, I was the master at opening conversations with girls, but then I would get too drunk and leave the bar to get food. Getting wasted at bars gets old fast. It's fun when it's new and exciting, but you realize the effects it has on your body and mind when you start getting closer to my age. After my car accident, I knew I had to slow down on the partying. I stopped hanging out with the party crowd and started trying to find friends that wanted to talk business ideas.

Many people would rather be part of a group and do what everyone else is doing rather than blazing their own path. The way I see it is, the school system ingrains this into their students. They say, "follow the Yellow Brick Road." Here's how I see it: go to college, have fun, get in debt, find a job out of school, and then pay back your loans for the next five years. Sounds like a *great* life. My parents would always say, "just be grateful you have a job and money coming in." That is not how I will live my life.

Many people want to be the leader but they feel they don't have the confidence to do so. The way I see it, self confidence is the most important part about becoming a leader.

Many people would rather do what their friends are doing rather than what they want to do because they can't say NO. The way I see it is, it's your life and you should only do what you want to do. Saying "NO" is hard but it feels great when you are able to stand your ground and not feel the effects of FOMO: the fear of missing out!

Screw you Kanye for making that a thing.

Here are the steps I took to get these results:

Start by looking at your friends:

Is this the group of friends you want to lead? If you feel likes it's too much of a challenge leading your friends, then maybe it's time to move on. Find friends that are interested in your passions. You can't force people to do what you want to do. They will only follow if they are generally interested.

Make more decisions:

It's good to create a democracy where different people are choosing where to go or what to do. Start by bringing this up and seeing what your friends say. Don't let the same person always decide where to go.

Plan something and sell it to your friends:

The more time you invest into the plan, the easier it is to sell. Your plan is much larger than just an idea. Your friends will be more inclined to go along with it and they will want to attend. I have an idea for your first event or party. Find a venue, get a good DJ, invite the opposite sex and tell your friends that there will be a lot of single people there. It's foolproof.

Be sure to avoid these common mistakes:

→ Going with the flow and doing stuff you don't really enjoy.

→ Hanging out with friends that aren't open to new things or interested in your passions.

→ Booking an event, but not doing any planning. You can't just wing it. You will lose your leadership credibility and that is hard to earn back.

Action Step:

Start by finding some events in your area that you would like to attend. Ask a couple of your friends if they would like to join. If they don't want to, go alone or sell them on the event. If they try and talk you out of going to the event, they don't support your passion. Move on. Go find new friends.

The Uneasy Man

Believe me when I say this: being a leader is much better than being a follower. If you are in a group of friends who never want to do what you do and you feel it's ruining your confidence then it's time to take action and get out.

Imagine you let a year go by and you are still hanging out with the same friends from high school. Eventually, you will wonder why you haven't excelled in life. You are the five people you hang around with most. If all five of your friends sit around smoking pot and never try to improve their life, then guess what? You'll do that too.

14. Master Body Language

"Confidence is not posting endless selfies, or repeatedly protesting how happy or in love we are, it's a subtle yet noticeable sheen that emanates from our being - our eyes, our words, our body language."
— Sam Owen, *500 Relationships And Life Quotes: Bite-Sized Advice For Busy People*

Have you ever been at a social event and felt everyone looked confident BUT YOU?

Have you ever heard that your body language can tell others a lot about your self-confidence?

Have you ever wanted to look confident while standing in line for coffee?

Same here my friend!

Your body language is one of the first things that will either attract someone to you or scare them off. You want to come off as confident, not an arrogant SOB!

In college, I thought I had my life in order. I was the captain of the volleyball team, I had this confidence about me that maybe came off as a little cocky. I couldn't help it, I didn't know any better. I was a gym-rat meathead who worked out everyday and wanted to get as big as I could because that's what I thought men did to become confident. The gym helped me increase my confidence on the surface but it wasn't helping my self-confidence. Gym confidence doesn't last and if you go six days a week, you will still feel like piece of trash for not going on your **only** day off. You start feeling like you need the 'pump' every single day. The gym made me feel good about myself for a couple of hours, but then the voice in my head would make me feel insecure and worried about my future again. I would go out on a Friday night and I thought girls would just talk to me cause I had big muscles, but now that I think off it, I probably came off as a jerk. I was a womanizer. I only wanted to have one night stands, so I could feel better about myself. I wanted someone to want me. I was good with girls after the initial meeting. Once, I got into the flow of things, I became relaxed and confident. In most cases, I would get so wasted that I couldn't even speak to women by the end and I would eventually end up going home alone with a burrito in my hand or going home with a random girl that gave me attention.

As I grew older, I lost interest in going to the gym everyday. I knew I had to find a way to increase my confidence without always having to go to the gym. I was tired of looking like a meathead that would get judged as soon as people saw me. I wanted people to not be intimidated, I wanted them to get to know me. I'd be rich if I had a nickle for every time someone said: "At first, I thought you were a dick, but as I got to talk to you, you're actually really nice." I wanted people to see me as fit, not a gym freak. I wanted to build my confidence from the inside out and finally be able to accept ME for who I am. I knew I was a genuine, thoughtful person on the inside but it took people time to notice that because of my appearance. I don't blame them - many people compared me to Lex Luthor. I started to do research into the world of body language. I didn't realize how much I had to improve! Wow! I started to do change my body language so people would think I looked confident rather than cocky.

Many people see a good looking guy in the bar and think he's confident because he looks like that, but you can be a good looking guy and still have *zero* confidence. The way I see it, your body language will speak volumes before you ever open your mouth.

Many people have never learned the basics of body language and the effect it can have. The way I see it, even a basic understanding of this idea can be hugely beneficial. There is something in the world of body language called power poses: it's powerful stuff. I will list them below.

Many people don't think twice about how they stand at a bar or in public, but the way I see it is, if they took a little time to focus on stronger body language, you will have much better results with meeting new people. Especially the opposite sex!

Here are the steps I took to get these results:
Learn these Power Poses:

Superman/Superwoman:
This one is my personal favorite as it's easy to do anywhere and still looks natural. Stand with your feet hip width apart and put your hands on your hips – and stand tall and remember to have a small bend in your knees.

The Winner:
This is the pose people take when they're proud of themselves for winning. To do this, again stand tall and place arms stretched completely out in the air.
Interestingly, research shows that people who are born blind from birth stick their proud hands in the air when winning a competition – thus, making this pose an innate pose of pride and power.

The Boss:
If you're sitting in a room before a meeting occurs, grab a minute or two to do this power pose. Sit back in your chair and stretch your arms out and place your hands behind your head, causing your elbows to be facing outward. Think of a boss and how they'd pose, they'd probably put

their feet up if possible, so if possible, do that too.

The Loomer:

Lean on the table and even stand over it a bit for added confidence. This might not be great to do in a meeting, unless it calls for it.

Improving your body language and learning power poses will help you raise your confidence in a social setting and people will start to look at you much different.

Imagine a year down the road and you still haven't improved your body language and you will be in the exact same position. Going out with friends and being the guy that just stands at the bar talking to his guy friends rather than talking to women. Start improving your confidence and you will start improving your life.

Action Step:

Take action right now and walk to the mirror and practice one of the poses that I listed above and find the one that works best for you. Which one will you use to master your body language.

15. Become A Smooth Talker

"The art of conversation is the art of hearing as well as of being heard."

- William Hazlitt,

Have you ever wanted to know how to keep ANY conversation going?

Have you ever felt like the majority of your conversations stay on the surface and they never dig deep enough?

Have you ever wanted to structure a conversation so it flows naturally?

Same here!
The art of conversation is an amazing skill to have that can improve your conversations at a networking event or with someone you are romantically attracted to.

I'm gonna quickly toot my own horn here and tell you that I'm good with people. I can create lasting relationships with people just by what I have learned throughout my life. I like to listen and ask questions about their life. I enjoy hearing people's stories. I think that's why I have always enjoyed bartending.

When you go to the events, you want to have amazing talks. They make the event feel like it was worth it. You want to get to know someone and really dig deep with them.

I felt my conversations always went deep if I was actually interested in what the other person was saying. More intricate questions came naturally. I would lead them down a path to tell me more. At first it wasn't structured, it just happened. I first learned how to lead a conversation from Dale Carnegie and I was intrigued that there was an actual way to lead people to a meaningful conversation.

I started to adapt my own way and here is the biggest tip I've learned for creating a meaningful connection: everyone's favourite subjects is themselves. They like to answer questions about themselves. No one will ever leave a conversation and say: "man, that was an annoying conversation, he just kept asking me questions about my life!" You can chime in with some answers, but let the focus be on the person you are talking with.

Many people see a conversation like a ping pong match; back and forth. The way I see it, it's like a game of hockey when you're on the powerplay. Keep the puck in their end as long as you can and once in awhile, they will dump the puck down to the your side and you can answer questions about yourself. You know you're Canadian when you relate a conversation to the game of hockey!

Many people think they have to impress the people they are talking with. The way I see it, be genuinely interested in what the person does and that will create a better connection in the end.

Many people think speaking for a long period of time is awkward but the way I see it, if you have a conversation map, you can get the most out of the conversation in the least amount of time.

Here are the steps I took to get these results:

Start with a compliment:
Be as specific as possible: "I like your shoes!" Starting with a genuine compliment will start the conversation on the right foot.

Embrace small talk:
Think about a conversation like driving a car. You must accelerate to top speed. Small talk lets you warm up the engine.

Be genuinely interested:

Don't cross your arms or let your eyes wander. Remember your body language and be interested in what they are saying. Keep eye contact. Here's a quick little tip; stare at one eye. It will be way easier to maintain eye contact.

Start with general questions and dive deeper as the conversations proceeds.

The more interested you are in what they do, the better your chances of staying in contact after the initial conversation.

The Conversation Stack:
This is a visual trick for remembering how to navigate through a successful conversation. This concept was created by Dale Carnegie. This will help you improve your confidence while talking with someone.
#1 – Remember that the number one thing people love to talk about is…THEMSELVES.
Visualize a huge brass name plate with your name on it.
#2 – The next easiest topic is where someone lives. For example, people in L.A. can talk about traffic for hours. Seriously.

Sitting atop that nameplate, visualize a big white house surrounded by a picket fence.

#3 – Another easy topic is the important people in our lives. Remember that families come in all shapes and sizes these days.

Peering through the window in that house, visualize a family playing a board game in front of a fireplace.

#4 – All the way down here at #4, we get to what people do for a living. Work is a large part of most people's lives.

At the top of that fireplace is a big white work glove with a tax return stapled to the side. (Sub YOUR item.)

#5 – Many people adore traveling and can talk about the trips they've taken for hours.

That big white work glove at the top of that fireplace is holding on to the tail of an airplane.

#6 – If you haven't gotten a hit from the other topics, prepare to hit big with this one: Leisure and Hobbies!

On the right-hand wing of that airplane, visualize a set of golf clubs and a tennis racket.

#7 – Finally, there are people who just love to discuss concepts. They think cool thoughts; they want to SHARE them.

On the left-hand wing of that airplane, visualize a bunch of flashing fluorescent green lights.

Now before my introverts start hyperventilating that they'll sound like an FBI interview, let me give you an example of how this works. You might hit a great topic early on and never get to #7 in your "stack." But if you walk into a room KNOWING you know what to talk about, you'll sure feel a lot more confident.

Be sure to avoid these common mistakes:

- → Not letting them talk.
- → Not maintaining eye contact.
- → Not accelerating the conversation.

The art of conversation can help in many situations and you will feel much more confident next time you are at a networking or social event. Imagine you let a year go by and you are still having conversations like you are today. Take notice of how your conversations are going and learn to improve them! You could be building meaningful connections tomorrow if you just take action with this chapter.

Action Step:

Take action and adopt the metaphor that a conversation is like accelerating a car. Start a conversation today and be aware of how the conversation is flowing. Be patient with it and let it gradually accelerate. Next, learn the conversation stack. This will help guide through a smooth conversation with **NO HICCUPS**.

16. Find Your Style

"My mission in life is not merely to survive, but to thrive; and to do so with some passion, some compassion, some humor, and some style."

- Maya Angelou

Have you ever wanted to find a style that enhances your personality?

Have you ever wanted to stand out from your friends in a good way through your style?

Have you ever stood in the mirror for far too long trying to find what to wear?

As much as I don't want to admit, I've done all three. Finding a style was always important to me.

Growing up, I had an older sister who was very tough on me when it came to my style. I would finally find an outfit I wanted to wear for a date or a night out with friends and as I was leaving, she would say, "you're not wearing that, are you?" I'd reply with: "No Britt, I just enjoy walking around the house like this." This always made me second guess my outfit. I would just say "UGH" and go back downstairs to find something different.

The Uneasy Man

It's always easy picking on the younger sibling. If you ever had an older brother or sister then you know the feeling. If you are the oldest and you do that, fuck you (haha). The comments definitely made me self conscious and it *always* happened when I was just about to leave! I would always switch back to something more 'conventional.' I always felt weird for caring so much about what I wore and how I looked. I thought men were just supposed to throw on a shirt and run out the door. I cared about how I looked and I always wanted to look my best in public. Now, that I am older, I'm totally fine taking my time getting ready when the situation calls for it. Nowadays, I much more confident with just pulling a shirt from my closet and putting it on. My style has been simplified ever since moving to the islands. I grew up in a small town and fashion wasn't a huge priority for the men around there.

My style has evolved over the years. Montreal is known for their fashion. I had to step my game up. There are very good looking people that enjoy dressing up and going out. That is what I loved. In the first couple months, I felt insecure because of how everyone else dressed. It took me some time to improve my style and it was easier to wear flashy clothing when living in a city like Montreal. I started taking more chances with my style and getting more confident. I started to experiment with colours and accessories that made me feel confident. That's what it was all about. Feeling confident in something made a world of difference for me.

Many men have no clue about their style and they will just wear the first thing they find in their closet. The way I see it, you should wear something that makes you feel confident and enhances your personality.

Many people think men just wake up, comb their hair, throw on a shirt and go out. The way I see it, that is possible for men who have the self confidence and desire that "out of bed" look. For men who are building up their confidence, this can be a hard task.

Many people will find a style what they like and never sway from it. The way I see it, trends are always changing. You should try and take risks whenever you can and continue to expand your wardrobe and style.

Here are the steps I took to get these results:

What do you like?

This has a lot to do with finding your style. For some guys, it's easier to look good in anything you put on. Some guys were blessed with a body type that makes it look easy. Other guys need to wear something that compliments their body type and it can be much harder.

Dress for the life you want, not have:

This takes you back to the first exercise in this book, what is your perfect day? What job are you doing or how do you want to be portrayed in that business? Dress like that. Just because you're not making much money right now and living with your parents doesn't mean you have to dress like a slob. That's got to change. Start dressing like a winner now.

Dress to your interests:

Don't just dress like your friends to fit in. Don't be forgettable. Is there a certain music, movie or fashion that draws you in? Express that with your style. Women love style and if you are keeping up with the times, it will show them that you are a confident man.

Don't try too hard:

There is such thing as trying too hard when finding your style. Everything doesn't have to perfect. I was always like that. I wanted everything to be perfect and then I'd be scared to take a risk and move away from conventional. I started to make sure I looked good but I wanted it to come off as if I looked like this way all the time. You can do that by making your style look natural.

Be sure to avoid these common mistakes:

- → Dressing like everyone else.
- → Not taking risks with your style
- → Thinking that "finding your style" isn't important for improving your confidence.

Listen: you're growing up and you want to be taken more seriously. If you don't improve your style now, when will you actually take the time to do so?

Imagine you a let a year go by and you are still just wearing the first t-shirt you find? You may "pull it off," but if you want to start improving your style, taking risks is a sure way to build your confidence. I know you want to start acting like a confident man and turn some heads. You deserve it.

Action Step:

Make a list of the things you look good in. Do you like to wear a blazer, a button down or a t-shirt. What are some things you would like to be able to "pull off?"

Women, if you are reading this, what do you like to see men wear? Help them by telling them to put a little effort into their style! Women like men who care about how they look. Right?

17. Dress On A Budget

When you're dressing on a budget, simplicity is key.

- Ne-Yo

Have you ever wanted to improve your style but didn't have thousands of dollars to do so?

Have you ever wanted to minimize the clutter in your closet but you found it hard to discard old clothes?

Have you ever wanted to dress like a young professional, but didn't know where to start?

Me too.

All my life, I worked part time jobs and I've never struck it BIG, yet. I wanted give off the impression that I was confident and on my way. I had to learn how to look good without breaking the bank!

Like I mentioned in the previous chapters, Montreal helped me become the man I am today. The city has a reputation for fashion and I knew that was something I was lacking. After getting settled in Montreal, I knew I had to improve my style but I wasn't making great money so I had to find a way to look good without spending hundreds of dollars. As much as I would have liked to go to Banana Republic and splurge on new clothes, I had to find stores that still had quality stuff for a fraction of the price.

The only time I ever went to Banana Republic is when it was 40% off. It was easily the best deal in town. I wasn't looking to buy anything full price. I found department stores that had a quality clothes that weren't as expensive as a brand name store. I'm sure you already know about some of these stores. You can find brand name clothes that aren't full price. Yes, they may be older, but they still work for what you are trying to do. We will go into more detail about what to grab from these stores later in this chapter.

Many people will just go out to brand name stores and spend their whole paycheque on one outfit and think that's good enough. The way I see it, you can spend your money on one outfit or you can use that money to buy a variety of outfits.

Many men will just walk into a store and grab the first thing they see and think that's good enough. The way I see it, you have to differentiate yourself and buy clothes that make you look good and make you feel confident. Try on different things and take some chances. You can always return it if it makes you feel uncomfortable.

Many men won't shop at smaller stores because they believe people will judge them on the brand names they wear. The way I see it, if your friends are judging you on the brand names you are wearing, it's time to get new friends. Look good, feel good. Stop spending money on brand names to impress *them*.

Here are the steps I took to get these results:

Buy dark jeans:

I don't wear jeans as much as I used to. Mostly because I live in the Cayman Islands and it's *always* hot, but this is a staple for dressing well. A good pair of jeans can be the difference between looking like a professional man and looking sloppy.

Personally, I think slim fit is the best unless you have skinny legs.

Make sure they're dark washed because this makes it easy to build a variety of different looks.

Buy a black or brown set:

A 'set' is a belt and shoes. Black is more traditional. You can go out and buy a pair of black shoes, black belt and dark jeans and you have already improved your style substantially.

Buy multiple shirts:

Now that you have bought some jeans and shoes, you want to buy some shirts so you can change up your style. You can wear the same jeans night after night. Switch up the shirt and you are a new man. When you are first starting out, stay simple. Wear a couple of high quality v-necks (black and white) and a couple of dress shirts (iron free). Once you build a foundation, you can start to expand your wardrobe with different colours and styles.

Accessories:

Personally, I like to keep this simple. I will never walk around with chains and a bunch of bracelets. Find a nice necklace, bracelet or a watch. Feel free to wear all three.

Shop smart:

You can find some great deals when you subscribe to different mailing lists. You will get newsletters emailed to you and you can probably get a good amount off the clothes in store or online.

Look for stores in your area that carry a variety of different brands that aren't listed at full price. This is a great place to go because you can find brand name clothing that isn't too inflated in price.

If you prefer shopping at brand name stores, don't just walk into the most expensive store. Find smaller brand names that offer high quality clothing.

Be sure to avoid these common mistakes:

→ Spending hundreds of dollars of one outfit.
→ Buying big brand name to impress people.

➜ Thinking you have to have the newest stuff to be cool.

So there you have it! Now you have some knowledge about dressing on a budget. Imagine you let a couple months go by and you're still spending all of your money on big brand names. There's a good chance you may grow out of it, lose or gain some weight and then you're stuck with an expensive outfit that you can't wear. Start using your money to build a variety of outfits that look good and make you feel good.

Action Step:

Take action right now and go look at your closet. Discard the things you don't wear or you've grown out of. Get back to a simple closet. Find out what you still need to build a good foundation.

18. Improve Your Shoe Game

"It is totally impossible to be a well dressed man in cheap shoes"

- Hardy Amies

Have you ever heard that your shoes are the first thing people look at?

Have you ever wanted to know how to properly maintain your shoes?

Have you ever bought shoes but felt they were impractical?

Me too.

Let's face it. Shoes can tell you a lot about a man. He can have the nicest suit on but if his shoes are worn out and ugly then his look just went down the drain. Take pride in your shoes.

Back when I was a young lad, it was all about getting attention from my peers. You didn't buy shoes for how they felt on your feet, you bought them to turn heads when you were walking down the hallway. That's what mattered to me at that age. I have always been a shoe guy.

The Uneasy Man

I had many different styles, I never took the best care of them, but I am much better than I used to be.

Having a shoe closet is big thing for a man. We need shoes for all different types of events. Yes, women are known to love shoes more than men but there are some men that could challenge them for that title!

You want to have shoes for different activities. Don't be the guy who wears that one pair of sneakers for multiple activities and events. There is no style there. Have a shoe that you can wear to parties, events and then have a shoe you can wear for casual dates or casual nights out. Start to improve your shoe game.

I never believed that your shoes are the first thing people look at, but you'd be surprised at how many people start at the bottom and work their way up. If the first thing they see is an old pair of shoes that haven't been maintained than you are off on the wrong foot. No pun intended!

Many people don't understand how important shoes are for men. The way I see it, men like shoes just as much as women, most men just don't buy hundreds of pairs in the same style.

Many men only have one or two pairs of shoes that they think they can just wear over and over. The way I see it, shoes are one of the first thing people look at. Wear a nice pair of shoes and you will start things off on the right foot. Pun intended!

Many people think shoe shopping is for women. The way I see it, you don't have to call it shoe shopping. You know what you want: walk into the mall, try on a couple pairs and buy one. It's that simple.

Here are the steps I took get these results:

Think about the functions you attend:

First off, you need to think about the functions you attend already and the functions you would like to attend in the next year. You want to buy a shoe that will be versatile. Find a shoe that can be worn to a formal event, but also dress down when you are going to a more casual event.

Clear out your shoe rack:

Take some time and discard any shoes that you wore in your 'wannabe rapper' days. Those days are behind us. Start cleaning out all the shoes that you can't see yourself wearing anymore. Keep the shoes that you still wear.

Active, casual & formal:

Three pairs of shoes is a great starting point for your shoe game. I like to have one pair for any sporting events I do, a casual pair for when I want to wear a nice pair of denim jeans and the dress shoe when I want to step up my game.

Think simple

You don't have to buy the most outlandish shoe because you may not wear them as much as you think you might. Look for a pair that is classy, but isn't over the top. You can shop for brand name shoes at department stores or even online.

Avoid these common mistakes:

→ Having only one pair of shoes for multiple events.
→ Wearing ugly, worn out shoes to a networking event.
→ Spending all day trying on different shoes.

The whole idea of this book is to help you become confident and even though buying shoes may feel like it doesn't belong, it does. Having a great shoe game will increase your confidence. If you only have one pair of shoes that you wear everywhere, it's time to change. Don't let another month go by like that.

Action Step:

Take action right now and go clear out your shoe closet and only keep shoes that suit your life right now. Find a shoe that you can wear to multiple events and aren't worn down to the sole.

19. Dress Like A Stud

The first step to being respected is looking respectable

- Unknown

Have you left buying a suit until the last minute and had no idea how to buy one?

Have you ever wanted to buy a blazer, but felt it wasn't practical for your lifestyle?

Have you ever felt completely out of place when you walk into a suit store?

I've been there as well.

Now, that you know some information on finding your style it's time to start understanding the world of formal wear.

Growing up, there was a lot of confusion on when to wear a suit and when not too. I always enjoyed looking my best, but I felt I didn't know anything about the suit game. When I was living in Montreal, I wanted to find a sports jacket I could wear that was inexpensive but still gave off the impression that I knew what I was doing. You see, in Montreal, my first job was as a club promoter for the nightclubs that needed help attracting people. I didn't have much money, but I had a confident look and a strong voice. You had to look respectable or people would just walk right by you. This job taught me a lot about rejection. I had people call me every name in the book.

Before this job, I never bought a blazer because I felt you could just wear a suit jacket and you'd be fine. Blazer's fit a little differently and they don't have to match your bottoms. You can wear a nice pair of dark denim jeans with a blazer and it looks great. I fell in love with my first blazer and I wore it every weekend.

Once winter came around, I didn't want to stand outside in a winter jacket promoting clubs, so I found a job indoors. It was telemarketing. I'd never made a cold call in my life. That was about to change! In the first week, I made an average of 400 cold calls per day and I didn't think I was going to last. Doing club promotions helped me stomach rejection a little better. The number of people that hung up on me was astronomical. I didn't have to wear a suit to this job, but I wore my blazer and it fit right into the perception I wanted to give off. Once I began making a bit of money at the telemarketing job, I decided I wanted to buy a new suit to wear around since I was getting promoted to higher positions and wanted to be taken more seriously. I went into a suit shop in town and the sales clerk taught me a lot about buying a suit, which I will share with you. I learned a lot about what size I was, what colours look good on me and some colour schemes that I never would have thought went together. I left that store with two brand new suits and a world full of confidence.

Many men will just walk into a suit store and grab one off the shelf and think that it's good enough. The way I see it, even if you buy one off the shelf, take it to the tailor and have him fit it to your body. It will feel much better.

Many men have no idea how to buy a suit or a blazer so they never do. I think wearing a pair of dress pants and a button-down shirt looks very sloppy. The way I see it, every man should own a sports jacket or a suit. You never know when you will need one and you can't keep borrowing your dad's jacket for the rest of your life.

Many men think buying a suit jacket or blazer is way to "dressy." The way I see it, a well fitted jacket can be very casual and it's much classier than just wearing a dress shirt.

Here are the steps I took to get these results:

Pick your attire:

This is what you must decide first. Do you want to buy a full suit that you can wear to formal events or do you want a jacket that you can wear on the town?

You don't have to spend too much. Don't worry too much about all the details. The buttons, the brand name, colour of the lining. All you have to worry is about is the quality of the fabric and elegance of the fit.

Fitting the suit:

A good suit hugs your shoulders. Be sure the lining sits right on the edge of your shoulder. This is the focal point of a suit. The chest on a good suit has a nice roundness and fullness to it. For sleeve length, you should be able to hold the fabric in your hands. It looks classier when the sleeves are longer rather than too short.

Tailoring your suit:

Fit is the most important feature. When you try on the suit, wear a good fitting shirt and a proper pair of shoes. This will help the tailor make the perfect fit. Show plenty of shirt cuff on the sleeves.

Proper suit care:

Don't use the outside pockets of your jacket, those are for show. Do not carry a backpack with a tailored jacket and do not stuff too much in your pockets. Be sure to take your suit to a dry cleaner: if your suit isn't dirty, don't ask for a wash. Let the dry cleaner know that you just want a press. I learned the hard way when I kept paying an arm and leg every time I got home from an event and forgot to hang my suit up.

Avoid these common mistakes:

→ Buying a suit off the rack and leaving the store.

→ Thinking you don't need a suit.

→ Not taking proper care of your suit.

Buying a suit that fits well will make a world of difference. Feeling classy in a suit is a great way to master your confidence.

Imagine you let another couple months go by and you still haven't bought yourself a suit and you are the guy showing up at fancy gatherings in just a dress shirt and wondering why people won't take you serious when you say, "I'm an entrepreneur looking for investors."

Action Step:

Decide if you want to buy a full suit or a nice jacket to wear out. Think about the budget you have to work with and the functions you will attend. Head over to your local suit shop and ask questions. The sales clerks are there to help.

20. Adopt Proper Grooming Techniques

Good grooming is integral and impeccable style is a must. If you don't look the part, no one will want to give you time or money

- Daymond John

Have you ever wanted to know more about proper grooming methods?

Have you ever wanted use products that will maximize your confidence?

Have you ever wanted to know the 'must have' products for men?

Well, Me too.

There are so many different products out there and it can be hard to know what you need to maximize your confidence as a man. Don't worry, I'll do my best to show you the ropes. I'm not even going to try and tackle what women need because I have no clue where to start!

Let's face it. Grooming can be somewhat obvious, but you would be surprised at how many people ignore daily hygiene. I'm not here to tell you to shower and brush your teeth. I want to dig a little deeper into grooming. I have already assumed that if you have bought this book, you know the importance of daily hygiene.

There is nothing like a fresh haircut or nice shave if you can grow facial hair. A great way to gain a quick confidence fix is walking into your local barbershop and getting a little touch up, but be careful!

Depending on how good the barber is, you may walk out feeling a little more insecure than when you walked in!

For years, I always wanted to grow out my hair, but there are awkward stages that I would have to go through. I would always get so far and then I would look into the mirror and I couldn't take it anymore, so I would just get it cut off. I finally made the commitment to myself that I would grow my hair out even if I felt completely insecure. Luckily, I had a great barber back home that taught me tips on how to stay confident when growing out my hair. I finally got to a point where I had thick luscious hair and I felt really good about it. I went back to a more neutral haircut at the start of 2017 because I wanted a change and I was done with people asking me where I played hockey. But, now I live on a beach, so I think the natural beach flow is the way to go.

Okay, I'm finished with talking about my own hair.

Morning routines are important to me and looking my best makes me feel my best. I have always been interested in grooming products. I have used TONS of different hair gels, moisturizers and other grooming essentials that I feel I could give some some great advice on.

Many people don't realize how important grooming is. The way I see it, grooming can make a big difference between an amazing day and just an okay day.

Many people think if they shower, apply soap and deodorant, they're goof to go. The way I see it, those are the 'must do's.' You can can take your confidence a step farther by learning how to maximize your results through grooming.

Many men feel lost in drug stores because they have idea what to buy and they just look for the product that are on sale (the way I still buy my deodorant!). The way I see it, you have to experiment with different products to find which works best for your face, skin and hair.

Here are the steps I took to get these results:

Skincare:

The first step we will learn about is something that I never saw a huge need for because I didn't grow up with oily skin. I obviously had zits that cropped up and gave me insecurity. I'm sure we can all relate to that.

What kind of skin do you have? Normal, dry, oily or a combination?

If you have normal skin than all you need to use is a gentle face wash and regular moisturizer (day and night).

If you have a dry skin then use mild, soap free face wash followed by richer, heavier moisturizer. Use a hydration mask and anti aging products so you don't get wrinkles too early.

If you born with oily skin than you may have a tougher time but it's not impossible to maintain. Use a cleanser with salicylic acid to unclog pores and reduce oil production and follow with an astringent toner. Moisturize with a light, oil free moisturizer during the day. As much as you would like to sit there and pick your pimples, try not too.

Shaving:

Shaving is a big step in a man's life and if your father never showed you how to do it than this may give you a little help (but not too much: I still can't grow a full beard!)

The first thing you have to do is prep your face. It's better to shave after a shower because that will open up the pores and make it easier to for hair removal.

Use unscented shave creams that don't leave your face dry. Apply using circular motion and use a brush to raise the hairs to get a better shave.

The next thing is go *with* the grain because if you don't, you will chance irritation and a rash. Use short strokes and rinse your razor frequently so you don't get a build up of hair.

After you are done shaving, use cold water to remove the excess shaving cream from your face and be sure to moisturize after or use aftershave because that will close the pores that open up during your shower. This will decrease your chances if getting zits after a shave.

Getting A Haircut:

Like I mentioned earlier, there is nothing better than receiving a great haircut. Not having a plan before walking into a barbershop could result in a bad experience.

Sometimes the best cut isn't getting a cut at all, so be critical. Do you need a cut or are you just having a bad hair day. There's a big difference. You have to be critical and make the decision that's going to benefit you in a couple days.

If you decide to get a haircut, take the time to look at different styles online that you like so you have an idea when the barber says, "what are you looking to do?" You can always tell your barber that you want your hair to look like Tom Cruise's and then show have a picture ready to show him.

Next, find a barber that you enjoy talking to and takes pride in their work. If you go to a really busy place that charges $15 a haircut, then they might not get your hair right and you'll have to deal with it because it's going to take a couple weeks to grow it back.

Don't settle for a cheap place. Find a barber that you can connect with and who actually cares about the finished product. A good barber will want to do a great job because if you are happy than you will tell your friends about them which will lead to more business for them.

One thing to remember is don't be afraid to speak up if you feel your barber doesn't understand what you are going for. Get them to explain it back to you and then you can tell them if it's right.

Be sure to avoid these common mistakes:

→ Not taking proper care of your skin.
→ Shaving against the grain and leaving a rash on your face.
→ Walking into a barber and asking for the special. Do some research before sitting down in the chair.

I know there was a lot to take in with this chapter, but this will help you improve your confidence because you are learning things that some men never really get the chance to learn. Take pride in how you look and you will ultimately feel much better about yourself.

Action Step:

The Uneasy Man

Think about which grooming technique you need to improve on. Is it your skincare, hair or daily hygiene? I hope this helps. Keep showering and applying deodorant.

21. Improve Your Love Life

Women are meant to be loved, not understood

- Oscar Wilde

Have you ever wished you could hear what women were thinking?

Have you ever wanted to know what you are doing wrong when it comes to women?

Have you ever sat around with friends, trying to come up with new ways to meet women?

I've been there!

THIS is one of the toughest topics on the face of the Earth to discuss because it's *very* hard to try and understand what women want. In my opinion, women want a man that has confidence in himself. That's not all they want, but I feel that's a great place to start.

I'm not going to sit here and tell you that I know *exactly* what women want because they are all different.

Trying to understand all women is utterly impossible. I'm sure women would say the same thing about men if they really knew how we think. Some women are attracted to different things in a man. It could be his build, personality, social status, his wealth and the list goes on. I'm going to go off what I have learned in my 26 years here on this planet and from the research I have done to help me attract the *one* girl that I haven't met yet (if you catch my drift).

I have never been one for relationships. I only had a couple of girlfriends in high school and they weren't serious. No girlfriends in college and no girlfriends since college. People sometimes ask my why that is? I say it's because I haven't found the one I'm looking for and I will know when that happens. I'm fully happy with my own company; I do not need to date the first person who gives me attention. I want someone who is going to be my best friend that keeps me accountable and pushes me towards my biggest dreams and aspirations. So, if you are women reading this and you think that could be you, send me a message!

I have never believed that two halves make a whole when it comes to relationships. I believe I'm already whole and I'm looking for another whole person who wants to take on the world together, as a team. That's who I want to spend my time with. Not someone who needs me every waking minute of the day.

You can fill a whole day looking through articles regarding "what women want" and you will get many different answers, but here's what I have found to be the most beneficial. I believe women want men that hold great potential. This could be potential of being a great lover, husband or loving father. They want someone who has a great foundation.

Here's what I found that women look for in a man. This list is not in a specific order.

→ Honesty
→ Trust
→ Loyalty
→ Social Status
→ Strength (mental & physical)
→ Security
→ Compassion
→ Romance
→ Caring

Here are the steps I took to get these results:

Love yourself:

No, this isn't a Justin Beiber song. One of the biggest lessons I have learned is that for someone to love you, you must first be able to love yourself. You have to be able to accept your flaws and believe that you are a catch and that any women would be lucky to have you. You can spend all day researching what women want but that won't bring one closer to you.

I only put the list above to show you what I have found while researching this topic, but the first thing you have to do is work on yourself.

Accept yourself:

As hard as that may be. You may not be where you want to be financially and maybe there are a lot of things that you don't like about yourself. You can still change how you see that. Accept yourself for where you are in your life. Stop thinking about the things you don't have and begin reminding yourself about all the things you DO have.

The one thing that made me more confident was finally letting all the things out that I let build up for years. I never used to like to talk about my feelings because I didn't want people to think I was weak or think that I was giving excuses for why I wasn't where I wanted to be in life.

Avoid these common mistakes:

→ Trying to act like someone you aren't to attract a woman you desire.
→ Beating yourself up because you aren't where you want to be.
→ Trying to solve your problems alone and not asking for help.

All I have to say is, be someone you are proud of and this book will help you in many more ways than just attracting women. That wasn't the focus of this book. This is aimed at helping individuals overcome their anxiety, stop worry, and attain authentic confidence.

Imagine you let a year go by and you are still trying to attract women by what you see your friends do or what you see in movies. Be someone you are proud of because at the end of the day that's the only thing that matters. Give someone a reason to love you.

Action Step:

Remove this thought from your head, "women want men who have a lot of money, are tall, handsome and have a good job." Those things don't hurt, but it's not the *only* thing that women want. Be a man with potential! Reading this book and implementing the strategies it suggests will move you closer to that.

22. Improve Your Relationships

To help yourself, you must be yourself. Be the best that you can be. When you make a mistake, learn from it, pick yourself up and move on

- Dave Pelzer

Have you ever felt like you are doing everything wrong when it comes to women?

Have you ever wanted to know what you could do better?

Have you ever felt so incompetent that you felt you are going to be single for the rest of your life?

So have I my friend!

When I first moved to Montreal, the first fear I wanted to overcome was being able to talk with pretty women at the bars. I felt that when I had alcohol in my system it was easier. I could talk to any girl and be okay with it, but doing this sober was a whole new mountain I wanted to climb. I remember I was at the gym one day and I met a bilingual guy named Sammi. I'd seen him before and we struck up a conversation. He told me what he did and I told him that I wanted to help people improve their confidence. He was pretty intrigued by that. I told him that one of my fears was talking with women when I was sober and he explained that he had had the same problem and that one of his friends was part of a company called *Real Social Dynamics.* This company helped men become more confident with women. I was interested in hearing more about this company, so I set up a meeting with his friend, Valentin.

I met with Valentin at a coffee shop in downtown Montreal and we started talking about how he went from a really shy, introverted guy to an outgoing, confident man that became really good with women. I heard the term 'pick-up' before only because I read *The Game: Penetrating the Secret Society of Pickup Artists* but I didn't think I would find someone that actually did this. He really sold it to me and I was interested in trying it out some of the methods he used.

We agreed to meet up and go out on the town. He told me he liked to go out three times a week, and hit up some bars in the area, but he never touched alcohol, which I found shocking. I didn't think It was possible to go to these clubs completely sober. I will never forget that first night. It was so damn awkward to be in a club sober! But, by the end of the night I was starting to get the hang of it. We went to a bar called *Foufones* in Montreal. I wanted to just walk to the bar and order a beer, but he told me try and do it sober. He said it will feel way better.

I accepted the challenge and went for it. I just had to be fearless and approach women. After I spoke to a few girls, I started becoming a bit more relaxed. I had some great conversations which I don't think I'd ever had at nightclubs because I was too drunk to remember.

After that night, I felt very accomplished for going at it alone and I decided I was going to keep doing this for a couple more weeks. It was so different for me. Instead of sitting in a corner drinking copious amounts of beer and watching women walk by, I was drinking water and just talking with any girl that came into my vicinity and man, was that a different feeling. I started becoming confident in a club when I was sober. Every night started off rough, but then it got easier by the end of the night. I met some very good looking women and they were shocked that I didn't drink. I felt they were impressed because I could be there, sober, and not give into the temptation to buy a drink.

Many people would find it impossible to go to a bar completely sober and talk with men or women. The way I see it, if you can manage to overcome this fear your confidence will soar.

Many men will go to a bar and **HAVE** to polish off a couple beers before they can even think of talking with a girl. The way I see it, you're not overcoming any fears by getting drunk and doing it because that is a temporary state.

Many men will spend the whole night looking at one girl but never actually talk with her because they were waiting for the perfect time. The way I see it, there will never be a perfect time to talk to that girl. You just have to do it.

Here are the steps I took to get these results:

Lower your reaction time:

This is one of the hardest things to do at first. The end goal is to be able to talk with women or man as fast as you possibly can without running over to them to say 'Hello.' You want to keep your reaction time low because if you wait too long, you will probably talk yourself out of approaching the whole night. We will talk about 'approaching' in the next chapter.

Don't try and be someone you're not:

This is very cliche, but it's so goddamn true. Don't 'try' to be a dick because your friend is a dick and gets girls. That might work for him, but it won't work for everyone. I once tried to start acting more dickish towards women and I ended up just scaring them away. I'm a nice, upbeat guy. I try my best to make women laugh as much as possible.

Intoxication:

Some people are more confident around the opposite sex when they have liquid courage, but when I drank a lot, my anxiety actually heightened and I was worse at speaking with women. If you are looking for just having a fun time, then alcohol might be your friend, but if you are actually trying to have a decent conversation and meet beautiful women then being wasted won't do you any good in these situations.

Ignoring her friends:

Okay, so you've met this beautiful women at the bar and conversation is flowing, but she has some friends around her that won't give you any space or alone time. Most guys will just stand there all night talking with the girl until she has to leave, but here's what I would do. If you talk to her friends, they will more inclined to give you some alone time when the time calls for it. There is nothing more annoying then trying to talk to a girl while her friend is saying, "let's go! We're leaving!"

Get her friends on your side and you will have more control.

Overthinking the initial conversation:

I hear it all the time: "Greg, I can't talk to that person. I don't know what to say." People seem to think you must have the the whole conversation planned out, but you don't! I taught you the conversation map earlier in the book and I have given you some great tips on becoming a smooth talker. You have access to the tools, you just need to go out and use them!

Limiting yourself:

Do not limit yourself to just meeting men and women at the bars. These places are a great place to start, but it's much easier to talk with women when they expect to be 'hit on' rather than in a public place like a park or grocery store. This is much more advanced than walking up to a girl in the bar. Trust me!

Asking too many questions:

I understand that I have told you that you must take charge of the conversation and put the spotlight on the other person, but DO NOT start firing off questions like you're on a game of Jeopardy. Use the conversation stack I showed you and guide the conversation down a smooth road.

Becoming too invested:

There's no bigger turnoff than someone who gets WAY too invested on the first night of meeting someone unless you two really hit it off. You spend the whole night talking, enjoying drinks, do some dancing and then he or she has to leave and you get all whiney because she isn't going home with you. You just met. Grab her number and do not send her a text right away. Wait for the morning.

Blaming yourself:

Here's a little dose of reality: not every girl or guy will like you. I hope this doesn't come off as a huge shock to you. I used to always do this. You cannot blame yourself if someone isn't interested in you. It is going to happen. There are so many factors that play into this and you can't allow one strike-out to ruin your momentum.

Be sure to avoid these common mistakes:

→ Just not approaching.
→ Getting too drunk.
→ Blaming yourself when a girl doesn't like you.

Approaching someone in a social setting is one of the biggest fears most people have. If you are committed to improving your confidence then this is a fear that you must overcome!

Imagine you let a year go by and you are still going to bars and getting too scared to talk with that one woman or man. Stop thinking about what to say and step up to the plate and take a swing. What's the worst thing that could happen?

Action Step:

Greg Rider

Pick a night this week that you will go out **sober**. Go along with a friend and tell them that you aren't drinking or convince some friends to all go out sober.

23. Overcome Approach Anxiety

"Approach anxiety is something every man has to deal with at one point in their life, If you don't deal with that discomfort you are never going to get better with woman."

\- Unknown

Have you ever been out at a social event and saw an attractive girl but couldn't muster the courage to walk up to them and just say hello?

Have you ever felt confident at the start of the day but then the fear of approaching someone ruined your whole day?

Have you ever wished you could walk up to any girl at any time of the day and say "Hey, how are you?"

Well, believe it or not, this is a huge fear for all men. I have heard many women say that they like when men walk up to them and start a conversation. I understand that we live in a very technology driven world where it's weird to actually have *real* conversations with *real* people that we haven't met through *Tinder* or *Bumble*.

This task is still hard for me on some days. It all depends on how my dopamine levels are. There are days when I'm in a good "flow" and I can talk with anyone, but then there are days when I literally think talking to a girl would kill me.

Throughout my life, people always thought I was confident and that I could start a conversation with anyone. I found it easy when I was just trying to impress the boys, but if I was out alone and I saw a girl I wanted to talk to, I couldn't do it. I think a lot of men can relate to that. We are always way more confident when we are surrounded by friends but when we are alone and vulnerable, we bottle up. I would always put on a confident exterior, but really I was very insecure about a lot of things. I would do things that I wasn't proud of just because it fit with that persona and it entertained people. I was in the gym five times a week, I played hockey, made fun of people, chewed tobacco and hooked up with women for the stories and not for the feeling. That's who I thought I was and the kind of life I would lead. This personna started to eat away at me as time went on.

When I was at bars, I felt like women would just judge me for the way I looked and I would attract women that I wasn't interested in. I knew there was a more humble side to me that wasn't being seen through the layers of muscle that I spent so much time building. Becoming better with women was something I wanted to do. I wanted to have the ability to attract women to me with my authentic confidence. I wanted to be completely honest, not use lines and be a great conversationalist that would give them a talk that they felt was rare and therefore feel inclined to stay.

I started to get way better at maintaining conversations. I would listen more than I would speak, I would be vulnerable about where I am in my life and I wouldn't try and put on a front to try and impress girls and it actually became very rewarding.

I wasn't really the kind of guy that loved one night stands. I actually loved having really good conversations and if I enjoyed my time with that girl than I would try to spend more time with her. I became a very smooth talker and I became confident when I had a girl in a one-on-one conversation.

Many men will try and put on a front, thinking that they have to "impress" women. The way I see it, if you are trying to be someone other than yourself you will come up short.

Many men have a lot of insecurities when it comes to women. The way I see it, the day you can start accepting your flaws is the day you will be more more confident around women.

Many men find it hard to be themselves around women because they feel they aren't interesting enough. The way I see it, if you take pride in yourself and are confident in your skin, no girl with find it boring.

Here are the steps I took to get these results:

Bask in the fear:

You must start looking at fears as something that you must overcome. This fear you have is standing in your way to becoming a more confident person. If that doesn't motivate you to go and talk with a girl or a guy at a bar then I don't know what will. You should say "Thank you for helping me grow." You are embarking on a new journey that will help your confidence increase substantially. It's okay to be afraid.

Take action in less than three seconds:

We will be lowering our reaction time dramatically. As soon as you see someone you want to talk to then make a line straight to them. It's about lowering your reaction time to under three seconds. See her or him and talk with them before you get in your own head.

Adjust after opening the conversation:

You don't have to brainstorm the 'perfect' conversation with anyone. Let the conversation flow naturally and adjust as the conversation proceeds. Use the conversation stack.

The Uneasy Man

Set the framework:

You are a man that is *interested* in her, Make that obvious. Use strong eye contact, deep vocal tonality and be physical in your approach.

Be sure to avoid these common mistakes:

- → Not taking action and letting your mind talk you out of it altogether.
- → Trying to eliminate this fear in one day. Be patient.
- → Giving up if the first encounter goes bad.

Honestly, being able to talk to anyone is a dream of mine that I'm still working towards. One day, I'm going to see my future wife walking down the street and I will stop her and start a conversation because I have been training for this moment. Don't let your dream partner walk by you.

Action Step:

Next time you're out with friends and you see the someone that grabs your attention, walk up to them and start a conversation. Feel the fear and make a conversation. If you lower your reaction time, it will be easier to talk with them.

24. Have Great Dates

The prospect of dating someone in her twenties becomes less appealing as you get older. At some point in your life, your tolerance level goes down and you realize that, with someone much younger, there's nothing really to talk about
— Clint Eastwood

Have you ever been in a great conversation with a girl, but didn't know how to ask her out?

Have you ever had an upcoming date with a girl but had no idea what to do?

Have you ever been on a date and didn't know how to take it to the next level?

Same here. Hitting the first date out of the park will make your chances for a second date increase. It's like a first interview and she has to be somewhat impressed.

When I was first starting out in the dating world, I would get incredibly nervous before dates (which is perfectly fine) because if you have feelings for a girl, you want it to go well. You always hear about what *not* to do on dates but never what to do. Should you take her for dinner on the first date? Do you just go for a drink? Grab a coffee? I never knew what to do.

I like to ease into the date and start with something that is inexpensive and quiet. You're probably thinking that is pretty 'cheap' but have you ever went out for dinner and felt so bored that you just wanted to leave? I have. I never want that again. You have to screen them and make sure there is actually some depth to the conversation. The beautiful thing is if you aren't interested in this girl, then you can end it after the cup of coffee and you didn't have to spend money on someone you are never going to see again.

I started to use this coffee approach for all my dates and it's worked pretty well for me. If the date went well, I would say let's go for a walk and then grab a drink. I hope the next girl I date isn't reading this because now you know my plan. Once I start to get feelings for the girl and we're comfortable around each other, then I'm totally fine with spending the money on a nice restaurant. Start with something small and get comfortable before jumping into a dinner. I'm not saying I'm the dating guru, but I have done extensive research into this topic and here is what I learned:

Greet her with a touch:

This can be a small graze on the arm or a hug. If this isn't your style, offer her your arm when you're walking somewhere. This will get you both comfortable with touching each other by the time you get to the chosen date spot.

Take control of the conversation:
In the first couple minutes, you should be the one that is talking the most. Launch into a story about yourself. This will allow her to relax a bit and get comfortable.

Keep the conversation light:

This is a great time for you both to get comfortable with your surroundings. You are just reminding her why she agreed to this date. This is your first date, let her hear your voice and have small chit chat before you dive into anything deep.

Use conversation hooks:

Starting the date off with a story will give her a bunch of hooks that she can chime in about. She will be able to ask you questions and once you've spent some time answering them, it's time to switch the focus onto her.

Ask her about her job and what she likes to do when she's not working.

Be in charge:

You're the man in this relationship and you are most likely the one that asked her out, so you should have an idea of what you are going to do. Don't ask "what do you feel like doing?" Women like a man who has thought about a plan beforehand.

One of the worst ways to start a date is ask "what should we do?" Take control and lead her. Take her to a unique place that you can actually hear each other speak. Don't go to the movies or a busy bar. Start somewhere calm and escalate from there.

Go to several venues:

This is a very important part of a good date. If you go to two or three different places, she will feel like she has known you for longer than if you just stayed in one restaurant the whole time. Keep it interesting and keep escalating the date. The coffee shop is great way to get to know each other and then you can go somewhere more playful like an arcade or a walk and then you can finish the date off at a nice bar where you can have a couple drinks. This is when you can start to be romantic and seductive, if you're feeling each other, of course.

By this time, if you have followed the steps outlined above, things are probably looking pretty good. You have had a great conversation, had fun, and you are both relaxed.

Go for the kiss:

This is can be one of the most exciting and scariest times of the night. It's important to not lunge in for the kiss. I used to lunge and it either worked really well or went really bad. I stopped leaving it up to chance and I started saying in a playful way as we're talking: "Just so you know, I'm probably gonna try and kiss you in a bit so I hope you're okay with that." This will tell you if she wants to or if she's not ready for it. If she's not ready for it, at least you asked. Thank for her going out with you and end the date.

Be sure to avoid these common mistakes:

→ Having small talk the whole night.
→ Spending the whole night at one location.
→ Asking what she would like to do instead of crafting a plan.

How many of those things are you currently doing on your dates? If you aren't doing any of those then it's time to refocus because if you are wondering why you can get a bunch of first dates and no second dates then I think we have found the problem.

Imagine you continue to date the way you have always done. Yes, you are going on dates, but you're not having *great* dates.

Action Step:

Think about your next date. If you don't have one, ask a girl out. List three places in your town that you think would like to take your date. Think quiet to start, playful in the middle and romantic in the end.

25. Get A Second Date

If you kiss on the first date and it's not right then there will be no second date. Sometimes it's better to hold out and not kiss for a long time. I am strong believer in kissing being very intimate, and the minute you kiss, the floodgates open for everything else.

-Jennifer Lopez

Have you ever finished a first date and then had no idea what to do after?

Have you ever heard that you shouldn't text a girl for several days after a date?

Have you ever invited a girl over to your place but then quickly got nervous because you didn't know how to get the place ready?

Well, same here.

My first time living without my parents was when I moved off to school for the first time. I lived in residence and luckily, I met my roommate during the summer while playing beach volleyball in Toronto. We found out we were going to the same college and we decided that we would room together. Mike was really good with the ladies and sometimes I felt inferior to him because he was a tall, muscular guy with abs and I was a slightly overweight guy that liked to drink beer and party. Really, I was an insecure guy that didn't really like who I was. I felt my roommate had a girl in his room every other night while I was alone in my bed and had to listen to them through the walls.

After that year, I moved into a student house with four other guys. That year started off great, but after several months under the same roof with four other guys, things start to bother you. Now, I'm going to be honest. I'm not the cleanest. it's still something I'm working on. My past roommates who are reading this book are probably nodding their head right now. I will definitely hire a cleaning lady when I have my own place. If you see me cleaning, it's for one of two reasons: I have a girl coming over or my mother is visiting. Either way I want to get the best impression possible when they see my place for the first time. When I have a woman coming over, I spent a majority of the time cleaning the common area and bedroom. I usually spend so much time cleaning that I forget to get alcohol, snacks or activities to enjoy.

Getting a girl to feel comfortable with you enough to come over is a good step in your relationship because it shows you that she trusts you. Make sure you don't screw it up by letting her go into a washroom with urine all over the toilet seat.

You have to create an atmosphere that is warm and inviting and there should always be options. When you have a girl over, you want to have options. If she wants to watch movies, eat some food, listen to music, have a drink or play a board game, you must have those things accessible. Have things to do so you aren't forced to do something that she doesn't want to do. Then the awkwardness can make her uncomfortable and she may decide to go home.

Many men will just invite women over and not care about what the place looks like. The way I see it, she's a girl; they care about cleanliness and even if you are a great guy, it can be a huge turn off for women if your place is a mess.

Many men will just invite women over and use the old "let's watch a movie" routine. If a girl likes you enough, she will accept your offer. The way I see it, make a couple options, so she can choose which one she feels most comfortable with. Maybe she doesn't want to watch a movie in your bed quite yet.

Many men are so concerned about cleanliness they totally forget about the activities that they will do throughout the night (like me). The way I see it, cleanliness is very important, but once it's clean you have to know what you are going to be doing for the rest of the night.

Here are the steps I took to get these results:

Always be prepared:

This can mean a lot of things. Have the place prepared, have your roommates prepared that you have a girl coming over and if the night goes very well, you may end up in bed and you should always be prepared with some protection. Try not to leave them in your pockets or your mom will find them and place them in a very obvious place that will really embarrass you. My mom would always put them on top of the dryer.

Have music prepared because it's a great to set the mood and if you give her the option to pick a song, it will make her feel at ease faster then if you just play the music you like. No music can be pretty awkward.

Stock the fridge:

Keep a bottle of wine or champagne or something girly. Not all girls want to hang out, drink beer and watch sports. Give her an option and she will be much more impressed that you thought of her needs rather than just your own.

The bathroom:

Make sure your bathroom is clean. I can't tell you how important is because women love clean bathrooms. Make sure you put a nice scent in there. Having a clean bathroom is a sure way to keep her coming back.

The bedroom:

Buy nice sheets and do not have any evidence that another girl has been there. It won't go over well.

Having soft lights in your room will be more inviting than bright lights. A good trick I like to use is putting a coloured t-shirt over your lampshade which will act like a diffuser and give the room some warmth.

Escalate Throughout The Night:

This is very similar to a first date. Getting the first touch out of the way as soon as she comes in your door, will make it easier to touch her later. If you wait until the end of the night to touch her, you might feel very uneasy and end up just laying next to her and feel really awkward. Touch early and keep escalating.

Be sure to avoid these common mistakes:

> → Cleaning your place and not thinking about what you will do while she is there.
> → Not have music playing in the background.
> → Not cleaning your bathroom .

So how does all that sound? Straight-forward, right?

I hope this chapter will help you get prepared so you aren't leaving it until last minute, having her show up to find you have a nice sweat on from running around getting the place ready.

Start taking pride in your pad and making it a great spot to have women over. Imagine you continue to do what you're doing and your nights always end in a hug and an "I'll talk to you later." Give yourself a good chance by getting your pad ready. This will give you the confidence you need to invite women back and not feel embarrassed about what your place looks like.

Action Step:

The next time you have a girl coming over for the night, think about what we just talked about. Clean your place, stock up on drinks and snacks, find a good playlist and think about activities you can do throughout the night. Being prepared will lead to a much smoother evening.

26. Craft Your Story

"Your life is a book; make it a bestseller."

— Shanon Grey

Have you ever told yourself that you don't have a story?

Have you ever wished that something bad would happen to you just so you could have a really good story?

Have you wished you could think back on your childhood and pull out these incredible life lessons?

Same here.

As much as you might not believe this, we all have a story. We all have a story that can inspire one, ten, a hundred or even thousands of people. Your story is unique to you and it has made you the person you are today. It all comes down to delivering it in a powerful way.

The car crash I wrote about in the beginning of the book is my defining moment. I like to start with that story because it describes the definitive moment in my life and how much it changed me as a person.

The opening line is "when I was 21, I walked away from a six-car accident that changed my life forever."

That grabs the audience's attention because they want to know if it's actually true? Was I injured? How did it happen? You want the audience to have questions that you can then answer throughout your story. That will keep them interested until the very end.

Believe it or not, the story took me years to find and it didn't come easy. I thought it wasn't a good story because I didn't get injured. After diving deeper into the incident, I realized that the crash changed my life because it showed me that I needed to change some things in order to fulfill my dreams.

I discovered my car crash story when I was attending a storytelling conference in San Diego; I still remember sitting in the audience. The exercise was to reflect on your life and think about the stories that jump out at you as your "defining" moment. I started writing down memories and stories that came to my mind. I thought of every story *but* the car crash. I wanted to find something bigger than that and I neglected an enormous moment in my life story.

For some reason, I do some of my best thinking when I'm on an airplane. As I was flying home from that conference I started thinking about what happened after the crash. I realized that the car crash was the best thing that could have ever happened to me because It made me want to explore different passions and not settle for a "good enough" kind of life. I was a completely different person after the accident because I remember looking back at the car and thinking, "what if I died, how would I be remembered?" I didn't like the answer I came up with. I know life is short and I had to change the answer to that question before it was too late. I began to dedicate my life to personal growth so I could leave a legacy behind when I pass on.

Once I started to believe in my story, I started to love it and now every single talk I do, I always begin with the opening line I mentioned above. I have had people tell me that my story is amazing and I always get responses like, "wow, I never knew this about you" or "is that actually true?"

Everyone has a story waiting to be told.

Many people believe that they don't have a good story, but the way I see it everyone has a story worth telling, you just need to identify it and believe in it.

Many people never take the time to look back in their past because it's too painful, but the way I see it putting yourself through that pain of reflecting will help you heal and getting the story out will feel that much better and can even help someone who is going through the same thing.

Many people think that something really bad has to happen to you for you to have a good story - a story worth listening to. The way I see it, you can make the most boring story interesting in the way you tell it and all you have to do is act on the emotion of the audience.

Here are the steps I took to get these results:

Put yourself in the past:

Start by finding a quiet place where there will be no distractions. Put in some headphones, meditate and quiet your mind so you have space to reflect.

Go back to your childhood and begin writing down stories or "defining moments" that jump out at you. This is just a brainstorm, don't overthink it. Write down good ones; write down bad ones. Start getting some of these stories down on paper. You can sort through them later.

Once you have this list in front of you, it's time to circle three of the stories that pop out at you. The ones that you think are your defining moments. Think about how these stories made you into the person you are today.

Pick one that you want to focus on. I want you to start the process of writing this story. Once you know how to do it you can do the same for all three and create three powerful stories about your life.

The Uneasy Man

Write for an allotted time:

Take out a sheet of paper and a stopwatch. For the next seven minutes, I want you to write about the story you circled. Now, once that clock hits seven minutes, YOU MUST STOP! Now read what you've written.

Now, reset the stopwatch and put another seven minutes on the clock. Did you finish the whole story last time? If not, that means you need to get to the meat of the story FASTER. Leave out the fluff. We will use this 7 minutes to get more descriptive and cut out the fat. Once this is done, you will have a more polished story.

If you feel the second time through helped you, keep it. If you feel you could be even more descriptive than start the watch again and go for seven more minutes. We want to make this as descriptive as possible. The more specific, the more the audience will be able to relate to your defining moment.

Be sure to avoid these common mistakes:

- → Thinking you don't have a story.
- → Not looking back far enough in your life.
- → Staying on the surface when you start writing. Let the words bleed out of you.

Carving out your story will create confidence in yourself because there isn't any better feeling than believing that you have a story to tell.

Imagine you continue telling yourself that you don't have a story and let a year go by and you still haven't taken the time to craft your story. How would you feel?

Action Step:

Find a quiet place. I want you to explore your past for the next thirty minutes. Think back to when you were a kid and write down ten incidents that happened that could be your defining moment.

27. Get Stronger At Sales

"If people like you, they will listen to you, but if people trust you they will do business with you"

- Zig Ziglar

Have you ever wanted to learn how to sell?

Have you ever wished you could pick up the phone and cold call a business?

Have you ever wanted to knock on a door and sell whoever answers without breaking out in a cold sweat?

Me Too!

You want real confidence? Learn how to sell and watch what happens.

All my life, people said have that I am a *natural* at sales. I wasn't sure if I should take that as a good thing or bad. You see, I grew up with a father who was in sales and I saw how he lived his life and sales didn't interest me like that. He would always come home and complain about co-workers or customers. He showed me the life I didn't want to have. He showed me that it's a cutthroat industry and you have to put up with a lot of bullshit. I'd rather create my own product and sell my brand rather than sell someone else's.

People thought I would be good at sales because I was outgoing, personable and had a good look. I never wanted to do sales and I would always turn jobs down. The truth is, I was scared of rejection. If that's a fear you have, you *must* overcome it.

I didn't like to sell because I had a such a negative feeling towards it. I didn't want to be a grimy salesman that wouldn't take no for an answer. I can't stand pushy sales people.

When I moved to Montreal, hospitality wasn't an option because I didn't speak French and couldn't speak to the customers. I had to find another way to earn money. The first opportunity to come knocking was as a club promoter on Rue Saint-Laurent.

If I wanted to pay rent at the end of the month, I had to sell and I quickly had to overcome that fear of rejection. Popular clubs didn't need promotion. I had to promote the clubs that weren't as popular. It wasn't an easy sell most nights unless I was pitching tourists and they had no idea what was good or bad.

I got sweared at, ignored, laughed at and told to get a "real job" countless times. It was very tough to hear those things the first couple nights. I began to take rejection like a grain of salt and soon it didn't phase me. Being a club promoter made me more interested in gaining further sales experience. Once winter hit, I wasn't interested in promoting in the cold, so I wanted to move indoors to a sales job. I found a telemarketing job where I didn't need to speak French because we called companies in the United States.

I remember starting that job and wanting to quit the first day because of the amount of people who hung up on me. Some guy even went as far as lecturing me about my life and telling me I was a piece of shit for working a job like this. I wasn't going to take that and I started yelling back at him. That guy fired me up and I said "holy fuck, I'm done caring!"

I stuck with the job for about six months and managed to get promoted four times to one of the top positions in the company. I quit one day because I felt it was becoming mundane and I wanted a new challenge. Such a millennial thing to do!

Many people never learn how to sell because they are too afraid to get rejected. The way I see it, getting rejected is a part of life and the faster you can overcome the fear, the stronger you will be.

Many people think that being good at sales is a genetic thing: you're born good. The way I see it, being good at sales is a learnable skill. Yes, there some people that have more potential, but no one is naturally amazing at sales.

Many people wonder why they don't have confidence in themselves and why they always fall back in the same industry and never stretch themselves. The way I see it, sales is an incredible way to improve your self-confidence.

Here are the steps I took to get those results:

Gain experience:

A LOT of people will walk into a new sales job and think, "I have to make a lot of sales to make this successful!" This is actually the wrong thing to concentrate on. You are there to gain experience and grow as a person. If you make some sales along the way then congratulations! Don't just look at sales for the pay cheque.

Learn the language:

When it comes to sales, it's a completely different language. You have to learn techniques, jargon, pressure tactics, urgency, objections, soft closes, hard closes and so on. There is a lot to learn in the world of sales and the only way you can get the hang of it is learning the language and immersing yourself with the other sales guys and in your sales training. You need to learn your product knowledge and how the top sales leaders are selling. Hang out with those guys and you will rise faster than you ever thought you could.

Never give up:

The Uneasy Man

The reason most people don't like sales or give up on it is because they leave too early. Sales has a learning curve and if you aren't willing to ride the curve, then you won't reap the rewards that are coming your way. If you are starting a new sales job then there's a very good chance that you won't make your first sale on the first day. Don't let that be the reason you quit. Stick with it and move on to the next customer. It will get easier and you will be a professional in no time.

Sales makes the world go round. Learning how to actually sell something is one of the best things you can do to improve your confidence. After I started making sales I began walking around with a bit of swagger in my step and wanting to sell more because I didn't want the feeling to go away.

Be sure to avoid these common mistakes:

→ Never trying a sales job.
→ Working for the paycheque, not the experience.
→ Quitting too soon and not reaping the rewards.

Imagine you continue to push sales jobs away because you don't want sales to be your job for the rest of your life. Look at it as a chance to build up your confidence and eliminate your fear of rejection.

Action Step:

Search sales jobs in your area and start looking for one that you think could give you a lot of experience. Try and find a job that pays base plus commision when you are first starting out. Doing your first sales job on full commision could be very stressful!

28. Own The Stage

All the great speakers were bad speakers at first

- Ralph Waldo Emerson

Have you ever wanted to walk in front of a room of people with confidence and start speaking?

Have you ever made up a thousand excuses about why you can't be a good public speaker?

Have you ever thought you could be really good at public speaking if you learned some tips?

Me too.

To be honest, I have always enjoyed public speaking, mostly because I loved being the centre of attention. However, I only liked speaking when I really knew a topic. I didn't like speaking if I wasn't sure about something and could potentially make myself look like a fool.

Back in grade school, my school introduced speech day. This was some of my classmates least favorite day because they had to stand in front of the class for five minutes and speak about their topic. Personally, I liked this time of the year. I always got nervous before speaking but I enjoyed the feeling it gave me.

My mom and I would find a good topic and start working on these speeches like you have never seen. I think my mom actually enjoyed it more than I did because she was able to write my speeches and then I would practice them until I was blue in the face. I still remember all the speeches I did from grade four to eight.

I was very nervous for my first speech and I hated it! But, as the years went on, I got stronger and stronger and in my final year, I was the best public speaker in the area. I won for my entire school, then I won for the next division up with schools from the area and then I went to provincials and placed fourth! I had speeches down to a science, but once I got to high school, I stopped speaking as much and just wanted to be a 'cool' high school kid that played sports. Every single time there was some kind of class presentation, I thrived. I found my calling at an early age and it was speaking in front of people. To this day, I have spoke at elementary schools and high schools and I love it everytime. It's just a matter of time until I am holding my own seminars, speaking and performing in front of a sold out crowd!

Many people are frightened by public speaking. The way I see it, public speaking is an amazing way to build confidence. You are always going to be nervous, you just have to push past the fear!

Most people feel you have to be a natural at speaking. The way I see it, no one is a natural. Public speaking is a learnable skill that you will get better at if you have an interest in improving.

Most people think the fear comes from speaking in front of people. The way I see it, it's not the fear of speaking, it's the fear of what people will think. You are holding yourself very vulnerable by being in front of the room. Learn your topic and kill it.

Here are the steps I took to get those results:

Change the perspective:

Stop trying to be a great public speaker and just speak. The audience will enjoy your talk much more if you are relaxed and not trying to put on a show. You don't have to oversell your speech, just stand up straight, be confident and speak about your topic as if you are talking to a friend. One little thing I like to do is find someone in the audience that is smiling and just talk to them.

Stop trying to be perfect:

People have this idea that everyone has to be perfect and to be honest, I used to think this too. I felt if I screwed up ONE word then everyone would notice and people would hate my speech. Here's the thing though, no one notices the mistakes as much as you do. Just shake it off, laugh, smile and continue.

Visualize the stage:

This is something I was good at without even realizing I was doing it: I would practice in my mind. I could see myself presenting in front of the crowd and then walking back down and once it was time to do my speech, I felt like I was already there. Visualize the stage, the audience and you up there, absolutely nailing the speech.

Be disciplined:

This is one of the most important things and as much as you find it annoying to practice your speech, this will decrease any anxiety you have because you have prepared yourself and you know your topic. If you want to become an effective public speaker, you must treat this like a sport and practice everyday leading up to the big game.

Make it personal:

While speaking in front of an audience, try inserting an anecdote or joke about yourself. This will help the audience warm up to you because it helps them see into your life and it will also help put you at ease because you're talking about something that you know a lot about.

Speak to serve:

So far, you have delivered a good speech, now let's make this an amazing speech with these final two steps. When speaking, you want to do more than just inform the audience about a topic, you want to help them achieve their goals. What is the purpose of your speech? And what do you want the audience to take away. If an audience is intrigued to learn more than you have done a great job.

Leave them with anticipation:

The final step! Just like your favourite television shows leave you on the edge of your seat, you should im to make your speech shorter than the allotted time because it's better to end the speech when people are at the height of excitement rather than speaking until the audience is squirming in their seat waiting for it to finally end.

Avoid These Common Mistakes:

→ Thinking about the public when speaking.
→ Trying to be perfect.
→ No practicing and trying to wing it.

Becoming an effective public speaker is a great way to improve your confidence and following the steps noted above will help you to achieve this. Imagine you let a year go by and you're still scared to speak in front of people. You know that it will make you confident but you keep using the same excuses that hold you back. Stop saying you can't do this!

Action Step:

Go online to *Meetup* or find a *Toastmasters* meeting in your area. They are everywhere and I guarantee there is one in your town. Go to a meeting, its free!

29. Be An Expert In Your Field

"One of the best ways to influence people is to make them feel important."

— Roy T. Bennett

Have you ever felt people would respect you more if you were an expert in your field?

Have you ever wanted to learn how to brand yourself?

Have you ever wanted to make a big impact in other people's lives?

I'm with you there!

The reason I've written this book is to help young individuals improve their confidence so that they can go after any life they want and not feel like they're outcasts for wanting more.

I'll never forget the first time I saw Tony Robbins on stage. It wasn't live! I was at my grandma's house and Oprah was on. Robbins was a guest on the show. I'd heard about him before, but never really knew what he did. I watched as he moved on the stage and was able to captivate the audience with his words. I thought that he was incredible. I turned to my grandmother and said, "I want to do that."

The thing was, I had no idea what I was going to talk about! I didn't think I had a story because nothing crazy ever happened to me. I was born into a middle class family and I thought I had a regular childhood. I felt I had no story, no life experience and no purpose. Why would people ever listen to me?

I just wanted to speak. As the years went on, I started to become more involved with personal growth. I began to dedicate my life to finding what I would speak about if I got the chance to be on stage. I had a lot of self-doubt about what I was put on this earth to do. At first, I wanted to help adolescents strive towards their dreams, but I felt I couldn't teach that because I wasn't doing that myself. I always thought you had to be successful before you can teach. That's how society explains it: you must have the education, experience and respect before you can show people what to do. Although, what I have learned in the past couple years is you only have to be a couple steps ahead to be considered an expert to someone who knows nothing at all.

This philosophy changed the way I saw 'coaching.' There are still days when I wake up and I'm not as confident as I would like to be, but I have introduced habits into my life that make me wipe away the self-doubt and they're all here, in this book, for you! I can get myself out of a slump much faster than before and, maybe I'm not as successful as I want to be yet, but I know I can help people that are suffering from worry, anxiety and a lack of confidence or clarity in their life.

Many people think they have to be rich and famous before they can coach others. The way I see it, if you're being authentic with your audience and being honest about where you currently are then they won't feel like you are years ahead of them.

Many people are so confused with their lives but are too afraid to speak openly about it because they think it will make people think less of them. The way I see it, being open about your struggle is therapeutic and you will find it easier to relate with people who may be going through the same things.

Many people put a lot of pressure on themselves to succeed because they believe life is a sprint rather than a marathon. They believe the faster you make money, buy a home, get married, have kids the more respect they will get from their parents and peers. The way I see it, that couldn't be farther from the truth. I have learned to trust the process and that everyone's life goes at a different pace.

Here are the steps I took to get those results:

Change your perspective on the word expert:

An expert is defined as someone who has specialized knowledge, but the way I see it, an expert is someone that knows a skill you wish to learn and who you are willing to pay for their advice.

What can you do that others can't?

If you have a skill that people want to learn you have a specialized knowledge and you are considered an expert to that person. Becoming an expert in a specific niche will pay you much more handsomely than simply being good at a number of different topics.

Knowledge is power:

The more knowledge you have, the more influence you will have as an expert, and the more you are perceived as expert, the farther you can reach. Take the time to study your industry every day and continue to learn more so you can help even more people.

Find your voice:

Do you like to write, podcast, make videos or teach seminars? Whatever you like to do, use that to position yourself as an expert and take consistent action when updating it. Create some kind of weekly schedule where you are releasing new content directly related to your field.

Avoid These Common Mistakes:

- → Thinking that you have to be rich and famous to be an expert.
- → Not continuing to learn about your industry and thinking "you know enough."
- → Letting self-doubt stop you from sharing your gift.

Perceiving yourself as an expert in your field will be a HUGE confidence booster because you will start to think bigger and take even more action.

Imagine you continue to doubt yourself about your expertise in a field that you have dedicated your life too. You will continue to come up short. The day you start calling yourself an expert is the day your life will start to change for the better.

Action Step:

Tell yourself, "I am an expert in my field" and fill in this blank:

People would love to learn how to, how-not-to or about _____ from me!

30. Future Pace Your Life

"Your future depends on what you do today"

- Ghandi

Have you ever started a new project but then after a couple weeks you stopped because you lost focus?

Have you ever made a commitment to yourself that you will do a weekly action on a specific day for 3 months?

Have you ever wondered where you could be in your life and if you made the commitment to do one thing in your business everyday?

Same here!

I was always used to think back to when I was 21 and wonder: If I'd picked *one* thing and just worked on it everyday, where would I be today?

Everyone feels like they should be farther along in their life than they currently are. I was especially hard on myself. After my car crash, I made crazy big dreams that I wanted to complete by the age I am now. I'm not close at all to even experiencing what I wanted back then and why is that?

The Uneasy Man

I have never believed that I could have a life people only dream of. I would sit there and daydream about traveling the world, writing books, making videos, speaking on stage and inspiring people. I would feel energized with my vision, but to be honest, the people I couldn't explain these dreams to were the people I saw everyday: my friends and family. I couldn't explain it in words. My parent's took the conventional approach to life. They got a job, bought a house and raised a family. I do want that life eventually, but I want to a live a life of adventure before I decide to settle down.

I never want to grow up and say to myself "I wish I did that," or "I wish I just tried it." You have to give yourself a certain timeframe to go for something and if it doesn't work out then you go back to the drawing board. I never knew how to future pace a project and I'll explain what that means.

If you want to get better at something, then you have to practice daily, right? Now, imagine you do the same thing everyday for one or two months, do you think you will improve? I'm going to say yes.

Think about something you want to learn next and imagine you committed yourself to doing it everyday for a certain amount of time, how far along could you be?

It took me awhile to learn this concept because I always had so many things that I wanted to learn and I would get overwhelmed and wouldn't work on any! If you can't think of *one* thing that you want to do everyday then don't stress about it. Here's something you can future pace.

I want you to future pace your life. Until you find that one thing that you want to do everyday, focus on growing as a person everyday. Do one thing everyday that makes you grow as a person. Read, write, meet with a friend, write a song, do an act of kindness, give a compliment, smile at a stranger. These may seem like small things, but imagine you do something that makes you grow everyday for six months, how would you feel as a person?

Many people look at a new task and think about how much work they will have to do to get the end result. The way I see it, that's your anxiety taking control of your mind and if you only think of the end result, you will become overwhelmed and probably not get much done.

Many people want to learn a new skill but they give up if they don't see results in the first week. The way I see it, if you really want to learn that new skill, then future pace that skill for thirty days and then see how far you have came.

Many people are so content with their life because they pursue the skills that they know they already have and never try and put new tools in their tool box. The way I see it, that is why people start to feel like they are stagnant in their life. If you don't continue to challenge yourself then what are you spending your time doing?

Here are the steps I took to get those results:

Make a list:

The first thing to do is make a list of all the things that you would like to learn in the next year. You don't have to just think about work related things. Do you want to learn a new language? Learn a musical instrument? Learning a skill like this will help you grow faster than you have ever thought

Learn something that will bring you closer to your vision:

Having different skills in your repertoire will get you closer to being perceived as an expert. When it comes to your business or your work, are you looking to just get by or do you want to climb your way to the top? What skills do you lack that are holding you back from getting to your vision? Write those down.

Future Pace for 30 days:

Take a new challenge and do it everyday for 30 days. I found 30 to be the best number of days for future pacing because for one month, you will do this skill everyday. I have done many different 30 day challenges in my life including; no drinking, writing this book, learning yoga, learning guitar, songwriting, cold calling and more.

Be careful to avoid these common mistakes: Looking at the work it will take to learn a new skill.

→ Not future pacing it and just doing it when you feel like it.

→ Not making a list and doing the first thing you think of.

I hope this chapter inspired you to future pace the next skill you want to add to your tool belt. I always had a problem with learning new skills before I learned how to future pace something. This made the new skill feel less intimidating and I just tried to move the needle forward everyday until I got a good grasp on it.

Action Step:

Take out a new piece of paper and make a list of the things you want to learn this year. Now, narrow it down to a few that *really* interest you the most or will move you closer to your vision.

Congratulations! You made it through the book.

How do you feel?

We were pleasantly surprised at Christmas to receive a book written and published by our 27-year-old grandson. Greg lives in Nashville, home of the Grand Ole Opry, where he sings and plays guitar weekly at two clubs. He now happily refers to himself as a singer/songwriter.

We have books available for sale for $15 and can be reached at 519-751-2134.

The Uneasy Man

Conclusion

Well, that's a mic drop if I say so myself. As I'm writing this conclusion, I'm smiling at all the work I have done to complete this book. I've wanted to write a book for a couple of years, just to get my thoughts down and share my experiences. It took me years to believe that I was capable of writing this book.

The first thought that comes to my mind now is "will anyone actually read this?"

The truth is you never know. As much as I would love people to read this and get inspired to live a bigger life, this book is a huge accomplishment for me. Writing this book shows me that I am capable of doing great things If I choose to believe in myself and not listen to the haters around me who gave up on their dreams.

I hope you can take away from the different strategies that I used to dramatically improve my life and use them in your own. I feel I have learned a lot in my 26 years and I have gained an abundance of experience. Sometimes I don't give myself enough credit. I wanted to use as many personal stories as I possibly could to show you where I came from and where I am now. I am a man on a mission: I am getting closer to my vision everyday and so are you.

The Uneasy Man

Reading this book has given you a peek into how my mind works and how my life has been up to this point.

Now that you have learned about me, I want to learn about you. I will never give up on my dreams and I will never give up on yours either. We will never settle for a "good enough" life and we will continue to challenge ourselves everyday and grow into people we are proud of.

I wish you the best in everything and I can't wait until we connect in real life. Until then, connect with me here:

Facebook: Life Of Rider
Instagram: Lifeofrider_
Youtube: Life Of Rider

I'm glad you invested your time into reading my book. Now, I want to invest my time into you. I am offering a free 30-minute breakthrough call to help you get crystal clear on your vision, goals, and challenges. I will help you carve out your roadmap, shatter self-sabotage and build authentic confidence. Please send me a message through my Facebook and we can set up your call!

Chat soon.

Your friend,

Greg Rider Farrell

Made in the USA
Columbia, SC
24 January 2018